Famous Biographies for Young People

FAMOUS
NEGRO ATHLETES

FAMOUS
NEGRO ATHLETES

by Arna Bontemps

ILLUSTRATED WITH PHOTOGRAPHS

Dodd, Mead & Company · New York

FOR ALEX

CONTENTS

Illustrations follow page 64

FAMOUS
NEGRO ATHLETES

JOE LOUIS

[1914–   ]

THE STARS over Yankee Stadium had never seemed brighter,
or farther away, than on the night of June 25, 1935. Glancing
up at them, a quiet boy leaned forward in his seat, his shoul-
ders relaxed, a towel draped over his head like a hood. He was
wearing a blue silk robe and waiting for the preliminary fights
to end so that he could enter the ring for his first really important boxing match.

This is not to say that other fights had not been important.
All of them had been important, amateur and professional
alike, to a boy whose eyes were on the stars, who had chosen
boxing as his golden stairway. But the brightly illuminated
ring in the New York baseball park, the sixty thousand spectators in the darkness around it, the $375,000 they had paid at
the gate in admissions, and the millions of people across the
nation and overseas who waited before their radios for this
fight to begin meant the difference between small time and
big time, and it was enough to give a young newcomer but-
terflies, or stage fright.

His opponent too was something to be concerned about.

13

Sportswriters called him the Man Mountain. He was six feet six and weighed nearly three hundred pounds. Recently he had been heavyweight champion of the world, and he was still about as strong and dangerous as ever. But if the young Joe Louis worried about Primo Carnera, about the great crowd that packed the stadium or the greater audience before their radios, his face did not show it. One could not tell by looking at him what he was thinking. One could not even be sure that he was thinking at all.

But now the preliminaries were over, and he was in the ring. The Man Mountain faced him from a stool in the opposite corner, and the announcer had begun introducing celebrities from the audience. This completed, the announcer quieted the anxious crowd once more, paused, and then said into the microphone these rather unusual words for a boxing announcer:

"Ladies and gentlemen, tonight we have gathered here to watch a contest of athletic skill. We are Americans. That means that we have come from homes of many different faiths and that we represent a lot of different nationalities. In America we admire the athlete who can win by virtue of his skill. Let me then ask you to join me in the sincere wish that regardless of race, color or creed, the better man may emerge victorious. Thank you."

When the two boxers met in the center of the ring a few moments later, they wasted no time. Action was brisk from the start. Mainly, of course, this was preliminary action, feeling the opponent out, feinting, studying, but it could be seen that Louis was quicker than the towering Carnera and that his style of boxing was more polished. He could slip past the

14

other man's extended arms, pick off his punches before they could land, and at one point he handed Carnera a quick sample of his own punching power. A look of deep surprise came to the face of the Man Mountain as Joe Louis's left hook caught him. His jaw was still smarting from it when the first round ended, but Carnera's heart was big, and he playfully picked young Joe up in his arms and gave him a little toss toward his corner.

It was a sporting gesture on the giant's part, but Louis repaid him at one point in the second round by lifting the big man off his feet and swinging him around. Meanwhile Joe continued to box his opponent and to slip punches under and over the reaching arms that seemed to paw at him in return. While it was still too early to make a safe prediction, the trained eye of an experienced fight fan could see by the end of this stanza which way the signs pointed.

The third, fourth and fifth rounds repeated the pattern. As he warmed up and the pace quickened, the tiger-like grace of Louis's trim body became more and more apparent. His eyes narrowed, and his concentration seemed almost as intense as a mathematician's. He was hitting Carnera with both hands, but he was not unloading. He was working his man as a bull-fighter might do, studying his rhythm and measuring his jaw.

Carnera, however, kept threatening. The Goliath-like strength that had once earned him the heavyweight diadem was as awesome as ever. His power to shake his head and swing his mighty fists after taking blows that would have paralyzed most stalwarts was still evident. And he knew, as did everybody else, that in boxing as in life one mighty swing, one tremendous effort, can often equalize an otherwise unequal contest. So he lowered his head and lunged forward with bull-like fury.

As the sixth round opened, Primo roared across the ring in an attempt to nullify with main strength and awkwardness the sharpness and the boxing finesse of his lithe opponent. Joe Louis swerved enough to take some of the steam out of the rush. Then, as Carnera moved to recover balance and leaned forward to charge again, Joe's left hand exploded. The blast went to a spot Joe had been watching like a hawk for five careful, calculating rounds: Carnera's jaw. One spectator observed that a stone wall might have withstood it. But Carnera's jaw was not a stone wall. He dropped his guard. He rocked on his heels.

In the same second Joe's right hand gave off sparks as it went to the same spot. Carnera swayed and fell forward in the center of the ring. His body twisted as he lay on the canvas, but at the count of four he pulled himself up. His face had the expression of a man who had just returned from a long and unpleasant journey. He tried to raise his heavy arms, but Joe Louis would not give him time. Another right hand shook the tired ex-champion, and he toppled again. Once more he pulled himself up, staggering, and again young might thundered, and he went down. After the third knockdown Carnera was helpless, out on his feet, so referee Arthur Donovan stepped between the two men and signified that the fight was over.

Within seconds there was crowded confusion in the ring, but somehow the radio announcer managed to get his microphone in front of the calm, unperturbed winner. How did it feel? Did Carnera hurt him? Did Joe have anything to say? In a coarse voice but with irresistible sincerity the boy who was

16

more accustomed to talking with his hands than with his lips finally replied, "I glad I win."

The roaring crowd in Yankee Stadium missed this, but all over the United States colored folk sitting tensely before radios suddenly fell off their chairs with warm, fond laughter. Victory is always sweet when you are rooting for a contestant, but a winner who spoke their language and was not proud was practically irresistible. Joe Louis was *their* boy. According to one reporter, "Pandemonium broke loose" among these folk. "Tens of thousands marched through the streets," laughing, singing, weeping for a new hero. Some even went to church to pray.

The quiet, good-looking boy who was the cause of this vast emotional throb was born May 13, 1914, on an Alabama share farm near Lafayette in the Buckalew Mountain country. He was the fifth child of Monroe and Lilly Barrow. Two more children were born to the couple in the two years that followed, but by then the burden of making ends meet for his rapidly growing family on a worn-out tenant farm had begun to wear Monroe Barrow down. He began to have sick spells. While Joe was still a toddler, he broke down completely and was taken to an institution near Mobile, where he eventually died. His wife and children never saw him again.

Meanwhile, the sturdy widow assumed the responsibility of keeping her seven children alive—without money. But she wasted no time feeling sorry for herself. She was as strong as most men, and she could cut cordwood, handle the two-horse plow, pick cotton or pull fodder with the best of them. The older children worked with her in the fields under blazing Alabama suns. They brought in the cotton crop as usual, but

17

according to those who did the checking at the commissary this was just enough to pay for the family's housing. Mrs. Barrow and her young ones raised collard greens, green beans and corn for food. Relatives who were only slightly better off divided salt pork with them.

Joe Louis was helping in the field at the age of four, but he did not learn to talk till he was six, according to some recollections. He was nine when he began to read. In the short-term country school to which he was sent in Alabama, however, he was a model pupil in at least one respect: deportment. "My Joe was a good boy," his mother insisted, after his name had been heard around the world. Neither she nor Joe went along with the legend-makers who tried to picture him as a tough little kid who could lick all the bigger boys in the community. On the evidence, one has to believe his mother.

Keeping her hand on the plow, as the old song goes, she not only fed her children and tried to keep some kind of clothes on them, but got them all ready and took them to church regularly on Sunday. Along the way somehow her good qualities and her strength were seen and admired by a widower named Patrick Brooks. Pat had a family of children of his own, but he also had a plan in his mind for his future. He was aiming, he told Mrs. Barrow, to "leave out" for Detroit.

He had heard about good-paying jobs in the big automobile plants, and he could hardly wait to try his hand at that kind of work. So he and Lilly Barrow were married, and before long he was on his way north, leaving all the children of their combined families with his new wife. They did not hear much from him at first. Anxious months followed. Eventually, however, he got a job at Ford and sent for his wife and all the children.

It had been two years since he left them, and when they reached Detroit in 1924, Joe Louis was ten. He had just learned to write his name. His speech was so thick he could scarcely make himself understood to anyone outside the family. He needed school badly, and his mother started sending him right away. However, after four or five years in the elementary grades, trying patiently, often painfully, to close the almost hopeless gaps in his primary education, he found some words on his report card that he was happy to show his mother. "Good in manual training," the teacher had written. "This boy should be able to do something with his hands."

His mother's first thought, as she read the words and as her face brightened hopefully, was to buy her big handsome boy an inexpensive violin and let him start taking lessons. She tried this, in fact, but it could not have been long before she realized that this was probably not the sort of thing the teacher had in mind when she suggested his doing something with his hands.

Joe had already been doing a few things with his hands. He worked after school at odd jobs. This became especially necessary when the depression hit Detroit and Pat Brooks lost his job at Ford. Joe delivered ice, sold papers and collected scrap metal for sale. Even so, neither he nor the other working members of the family could earn enough to pay the rent and keep food on the table. For about a year they were on relief. This hurt Joe's pride, and he refused to regard the money from the Welfare Board as anything more than a loan to be repaid. "I want all my chil'ren to be decent," Mrs. Brooks has been quoted as saying. Joe apparently accepted that as his own code too. He took it to mean hard work, no cheating, no sponging. Always pay back in full. Never expect something for nothing. Never hit anybody who could not defend himself. *Decent* was the word.

Joe was on his way to a violin lesson when he stopped to talk to a boy he knew who had dropped out of school a year or two before. Thurston McKinney had found a way to pick up a little money despite the hard times. He told Joe that he was boxing as an amateur light heavyweight and as such had won the state championship of Michigan. Amateurs did not get money for fighting, of course, but were given merchandise checks. If the merchandise turned out to be something he did not need or want, he could sell it for cash.

To be sure, this was small pay, they agreed smiling, but Thurston suggsted that it beat violin playing which, he thought, "ain't nothing for a man to do." At that very minute, Thurston said, he was looking for a sparring partner. He wondered if Joe wouldn't want to come along to the Brewster Center Gymnasium and work out with him. After some hesitation Joe agreed.

For a while Thurston McKinney danced and jabbed and toyed with the boy who had never before had boxing gloves on. Even so, Joe's reflexes were perfect. "His body," someone has written, "seemed to have an intelligence independent of his mind." Suddenly his right hand darted. The amateur champion of Michigan reeled and would have fallen had not Joe caught him and held him up. When the cobwebs cleared, the older boy shook his head with admiration. "You way too good for school, man," he said to Joe. The next day Joe Louis put his violin on the shelf and joined the Brewster Center

Boxing Club.

But things seemed always to happen by twos. As Joe began fighting as an amateur for merchandise checks, he also got jobs. He worked as a lathe operator at Briggs for six dollars a week. Later he got a job at Ford, always bringing his wages to his mother for the family pool. Meanwhile he won the Detroit Golden Gloves in 1932. The following year he missed his first shot at the national amateur light heavyweight championship, but in the two years he fought as an amateur, while working at Ford for twenty-five dollars a week, Joe Louis appeared in fifty-four three-round contests and won forty-three by knockouts and seven on decisions. He lost four. The first of these was clear-cut. It came a few months after he began to box and showed he still had much to learn. But in his second and third losses Joe looked more impressive than the boxers who got the votes of the judges, and neither of these fighters was willing to face him again. The fourth loss he reversed in a return match.

By this time the sharp eyes of boxing connoisseurs had spotted the golden boy of Detroit. In April of 1934, when Joe fought his way to the national amateur light heavyweight championship in St. Louis, reporters called him the best amateur they had ever seen and began to speculate on his prospects as a professional. Two months later light heavyweight Joe Louis met heavyweight Joe Bauer in a match at Highland Park, Detroit. Bauer was good enough to become an amateur heavyweight champion later, but the young Joe Louis knocked him out before the first round was half over. Thousands cheered, but all that Joe got for this fight was a $7.50 credit check for merchandise. As usual, he turned this over to

21

his mother. As he did so, however, he reached a decision on a question that had been in the back of his mind.

John Roxborough, a Negro lawyer and insurance man, listened with interest to the earnest young boxer. He could understand Joe's reluctance to give up a job at Ford at that time, and he admired him for it, but he had also been a spectator at ringside in several of Joe Louis's amateur fights, and simple honesty compelled him to advise the boy that his prospects as a professional boxer looked good.

Better than fifty dollars a week? Joe wondered.

Roxborough nodded. Better than fifty dollars a week.

Well, would Roxborough become his manager?

Again the lawyer nodded. He would.

An unusual man in many ways, John Roxborough was by turn tough and sentimental, but he was also shrewd and imaginative. Moreover, as a light-skinned man from Louisiana, whom people did not always recognize as a Negro and who had often heard what some people said about colored folk when they thought none were listening, it had always done him good to help boys he thought might give the world a better impression of his people. He had helped many of them with little kindnesses like paying their gymnasium fees. Others he had helped to go away to school. But the prospects of Joe Louis filled him with excitement. His imagination went to work.

Here was a boy who, with luck, might go the distance. To promote such a career Roxborough would certainly need help. No Negro had worn the heavyweight crown since Jack Johnson. In the years since that wondrous boxer amazed the world with his ring prowess while he shocked a generation of

Americans with his escapades outside the ring, no Negro heavyweight had been permitted to fight for the title. Some sportswriters, harking back and recalling the experiences of Johnson, went so far as to predict that none ever would. Certainly the way Harry Wills, for example, was avoided by Jack Dempsey (though there is no indication that this was Dempsey's idea) spoke for itself. Roxborough was old enough to know the story by heart, and he had no illusions as to the built-in attitudes a Negro challenger would face if his star really became bright.

He was also convinced that here was a boy who had a chance to change all that, if anyone could. To promote such a career, however, would require a maximum of everything. The management, the handling of the boxer's affairs, would have to be outstanding. The same would go for his conditioning and training. But these combined were not more vital than the image their fighter gave, what he came to represent. He and everybody connected with him would have to rise above the sordid environment that has been known to prevail in boxing circles. Even though they were not angels themselves, the men who took the responsibility for such a project would have to realize that everything depended on it. Big stakes were involved, bigger perhaps than any of them had ever dreamed of.

The group Roxborough assembled for this moon shot included, in addition to himself and Joe, Julian Black and Jack Blackburn. An old friend of Roxborough's, Black was a Chicago real estate dealer. On the side he had occasionally managed fighters and promoted boxing. He would be the man out front when it came to making the matches and talking to

23

promoters and rival managers, when Roxborough thought it best to stay in the background and out of the picture. Jack Blackburn, called Chappie, had once been an outstanding welterweight, but he had been involved in trouble and had not been able to continue in boxing. He had since worked as a trainer and conditioner of boxers, and the attitude of the fight crowd was that he was just about the best in the business.

When Roxborough first mentioned Joe Louis to Julian Black, he said, "I've found a boy, a fighter. This fighter's a good boy. Not smart alecky. Modest."

Julian Black laughed. "I've never seen a good fighter yet who was modest."

"This boy is," Roxborough assured him. "We've just got to make white people know it."

"The way things are, that's going to take some doing," Black answered.

"I know the kind of boy he is. I've watched him. I've asked around. You find out what Jack Blackburn thinks of him as a fighter."

"I don't think Blackburn'll be for training a colored heavyweight in earnest."

"See," Roxborough insisted. "And, Julian, I want him trained for real, in earnest. I've got plans."

As Julian Black predicted, Jack Blackburn balked at the idea. "They ain't never gonna let another colored boy wear that crown," he muttered. But Chappie was no match for the likes of Julian Black and John Roxborough when it came to argument, and before long he was in the gymnasium with the young Joe Louis Barrow, whose ring name was now shortened to just Joe Louis, working tirelessly to prepare the newcomer for his professional debut.

When Black asked how they were coming along, Chappie had to admit, "He's just a natural-born fighter. He's fast to learn. You don't have to tell him the same thing twice. He seldom makes mistakes. We believe in letting the other fellow make mistakes and then taking advantage of them."

That was the strategy he drilled into Joe from the beginning, and Joe followed it to the letter in his first professional fight at Bacon Casino on the night of July 14, 1934. Jack Kracken, a tough downstate battler with some experience under his belt, was the opponent. Seeing Joe's boyishness and remembering that he was just out of the amateurs, Kracken came out ready to wind up a roundhouse right. When it whisked by, Joe countered with a left hook, and the heavyweight from Champaign went down for a nine count. When he was on his feet again, Joe punched him through the ropes and out of the ring. It took him fourteen seconds to get back in, and the referee would not let the dazed Kracken continue.

John Roxborough came into the dressing room afterwards and handed Joe $59, the whole purse. "You keep all this, son," he said. "When you earn big money, I'll take my bit then."

Though Joe's first professional purse was small, it did not seem insignificant in the depression year of 1934, and the fight itself enabled Joe to establish what may be a unique record. Joe's fight on the Bacon Casino card that night was the main event, even though it was his first go as a professional. As a result his record shows that he never boxed anything but main events in his whole professional career.

The following week he was back at Bacon again against a

stronger foe, and the result was similar, though the purse rose to $61. When Joe fought next, it was at Marigold Gardens, a larger club, and every seat was sold. Joe disposed of Larry Udell, of Minneapolis, in the second round that evening and collected $101. Jack Kranz, of Gary, Indiana, was Joe's fourth opponent as a pro and became the first to go the distance with the hard-fisted newcomer. He did it by holding and running, however, and local fans began calling for rougher competition.

The matchmakers gave it to them by signing Joe Louis to meet Buck Everett in his fifth fight. Everett had fought more than fifty professional fights. He had never been knocked out. He had defeated some highly rated heavyweights and had battled others to close decisions. The sportswriter for the *Chicago Daily News* observed, "No fighter who has been boxing in the pro ranks only two months, having only four fights, could have a greater test than Louis will endure in taking on a battler of the high caliber of Everett." But in the middle of the second round of this bout, fought before another capacity crowd, Joe caught his man with short punches, and Everett went down heavily—to stay. Everett's managers promptly claimed that a lucky punch had done it and demanded a return match. This was immediately granted and announced, but Everett himself got cold feet and took a runout pill, as they say. He failed to show up, and there was no fight that night. If anything more was needed to spotlight the young Louis in newspapers elsewhere, this did it. Detroit especially wanted to see the hometown boy.

Joe's feet were on the glory trail. After nine consecutive victories, all but two by knockouts, the cry for stiffer competition was again raised. A ranking fighter with an established name was demanded by the promoters, and Joe's handlers were agreeable. The result was a match pitting Louis against Stanley Poreda, a fighter who just two years earlier had whipped Primo Carnera, Tommy Loughran, Ernie Schaaf, Babe Hunt and Johnny Risko, all topnotchers and two of them ex-world champions. But Poreda was knocked out in the first round, and Joe began to move with quiet confidence among the best heavyweights in the ring. But when he was matched against Charley Massera, of Pittsburgh, sportswriters in Chicago predicted he would meet "just the type of scrapper to make Louis look bad." The *Chicago Tribune*'s man wrote, "The most ardent Louis fans will not be so certain he is a great fighter until after tonight's scrap."

The fight was held in the old Chicago Colosseum on November 30, and many of the leading figures in boxing were present, including Max Baer, then heavyweight champion of the world. He wanted a good look at the boy he might someday have to meet. Matchmakers and scouts from all over the country were on hand, and if they were looking for a scintillating star, few were disappointed. Working carefully through the first two rounds, wasting no motion, Joe hooked his man cleanly in the third round, whipped a right cross to the jaw, and that was it.

And from this time on Joe Louis was indeed a golden boy of boxing, his every match followed intently by a host of fans across the nation. His David-and-Goliath conquest of Carnera added immeasurably to the luster. It also set the scene for poignant drama to follow. First, however, there was another challenge to be met.

Max Baer was unpredictable, but his physical powers were enormous, and he had shown in his rise to the heavyweight championship that he could be devastating at times. Moreover he had flair and showmanship, but he had clowned too much in his recent fight with the serious James J. Braddock and let the title slip away from him. There were many who believed this playful giant could still unleash fury, and the seriousness of Baer's preparations for this make-or-break effort in an up-and-down career generated tremendous interest in his September appointment with Joe Louis at Yankee Stadium.

The Max Baer fight showed clearly what the rise of the handsome Brown Bomber, as he was now being called, had already done for the sport of boxing. Since the days when Jack Dempsey and Gene Tunney had fired the sporting world's imagination and drawn million-dollar gates to their memorable matches, boxing had lost much of its appeal. The great depression had, of course, been a factor. But the interest in young Joe sparked a terrific revival. Betting was so brisk that one authority estimated that $5,000,000 would change hands after the Louis-Baer fight. An eager crowd of 95,000 fans started pouring into the stadium in the afternoon. More than a thousand newspapermen were sent to cover the event. One hundred and thirty-one wires were leased to different papers and news services. Radio broadcasts were carried over 130 stations.

Nearly two thousand policemen were assigned to Yankee Stadium that night, but few disorders occurred. In the ringside audience were the governors of New York, Michigan, Connecticut, New Jersey and Maine, and the mayors of half a dozen large cities. With these assembled were prominent fig-

28

ures from all major sports, the entertainment world, Park Avenue and the professions. Someone remarked that the ringside looked like a small version of *Who's Who in America*. Among them sat an enchantingly beautiful girl in a bright green dress with a bundle of orchids in her arms. She was Marva Trotter, a Chicago secretary whose brunette beauty was something to conjure with. If she seemed radiant beyond words, it was because just a few minutes before coming to the stadium she and Joe Louis had been married in the apartment of friends a few blocks away on Edgecombe Avenue.

Marva glittered and smiled as Joe sat in his corner waiting for action. When it came, it came with a rush. Baer fought with more determination than he had shown in a long time, and his first blow landed on Joe Louis's jaw. It hurt. Joe boxed the rest of the round with caution. He did the same in the second, but after the bell ended the session, Baer hit him with another shocker. Joe did not protest. In the third round he began to exact payment for both. Working with fierce concentration, he began to nail his opponent with hard rights and lefts. Baer rocked and fell. He rocked and fell again under a second shower of blows. At the end of the third round the great Jack Dempsey, who was acting as Baer's second, had to leap into the ring and half-drag, half-carry his badly hurt boxer to his corner.

All that remained for the fourth round was a neat, clean ending. Joe provided it. After another brief skirmish, Joe's right flashed, and Baer was down and presently out. When he recovered, however, he showed true sportsmanship. "I have no excuse," he told the reporters. When they asked him about Joe Louis, he added, "He's a swell kid and a swell fighter."

When photographers followed him to the train station to take his picture as he left New York, Baer waved to them, but his last words were, "Good luck, Joe Louis."

After the Baer fight taxicabs could not move in Harlem for the crowds of people in the streets. The Brown Bomber from Detroit lifted the hearts of colored America as they had seldom been lifted since the Emancipation Proclamation. Curiously, the boy who had not learned to speak till he was six years old was sharply sensitive to this. "If I ever does something to let my people down," he said, "I wanna die."

But the Max Baer fight, with its romantic sidelight and the satisfaction it gave to all those who had been waiting for a really exciting boxer who could lift the sport out of the doldrums, was actually prologue to bitter defeat and a triumphant return. It did not happen immediately. Joe kept busy, as a young boxer must to stay sharp, and he continued to win against the strongest opponents available, but the challenge that stung came from across the sea. Max Schmeling of Germany, beetle-browed and stern, an intelligent, methodical fighter and a dangerous puncher, had once been heavyweight champion of the world. Knocked out by Max Baer, the Black Uhlan, as he was sometimes called, yearned to regain the crown he had lost. He had started an impressive comeback abroad.

By this time, however, Joe Louis was a contender that James J. Braddock, the reigning champion, could not ignore. Accordingly, Braddock's manager announced that the champion's next opponent would have to come by Joe. This gave a special angle to the Yankee Stadium meeting between Louis and Schmeling in June of 1936, for despite Joe's meteoric rise there remained doubt in the minds of millions that he would be given a chance to fight for the championship. A victory over Schmeling would make it practically impossible to dispute his claim.

What chance did the thirty-year-old Schmeling think he had against young Joe?

"Louis can be beaten," Schmeling said unsmiling. "What the others did wrong, I will do right. I know Louis's weakness. He is wide open to a right, and I'll beat him with that punch."

The reports from Joe's camp, meanwhile, were a little bit disturbing. He had not looked his best to some observers, but these comments were brushed aside. You hear everything prior to a big fight. Moreover, the fight had to be postponed due to rain. When it was finally held, it started out according to the book: Joe Louis the talented boxer, Schmeling almost awkward by comparison but ringwise and carrying a blast of dynamite in his right hand.

But in the fourth round, when Joe should have had his plodding opponent ready for the moment of truth, it was Schmeling who unloaded first, and Joe Louis went down amid bedlam around the ring and in the stands. On his feet again, Joe was visibly hurt, and Schmeling poured it on. Joe never recovered completely. He boxed by instinct. At the end of the fifth round the crowd was roaring so madly neither Schmeling nor the referee heard the bell, and Schmeling actually landed after the gong a punch which, according to some reporters, played a part in the final victory.

Joe Louis was in a state of collapse as the fifth round ended. In the sixth round Schmeling put him down five times. Still

Joe continued to rise and to fight back. Indeed, a few rounds later it began to seem that Max might have punched himself out against his determined young foe, but in the twelfth round he finally came through with the blow that ended it. Joe Louis went down, rolled over and did not regain his feet till "ten" had been counted.

Joe Louis went to his dressing room bruised and disconsolate. "What happened?" he asked Jack Blackburn.

The trainer shook his head philosophically. "You got tagged. That's all—there ain't no more. You got in a low one too, but you didn't know what you was doing," he added. At this Joe pulled himself up from the rubdown table and turned to Roxborough. "You go tell him I'm sorry," he said. "I don't wanna foul nobody." Roxborough carried the message immediately.

"I hit him with everything I had, and he kept coming on for more," Schmeling said afterward. Amid a chorus of praise he added, "I don't think I have ever been happier in my life."

Part of the praise was contained in a cable from Dr. Paul Goebbels. It read: "To your wonderful victory my best congratulations. I know you fought for Germany; that it's a German victory. We are proud of you. Heil Hitler. Regards."

The Joe Louis myth had been exploded, some said. The government of Adolf Hitler made propaganda of it. Whether or not this stung Joe Louis personally, it did tend to highlight his role as an American athlete and a representative of his country. Soon many of those who screamed their lungs out as Schmeling punched him senseless in Yankee Stadium were quietly taking his side. Within a month he was in training for a comeback. Before the summer was over, he was in the ring with Jack Sharkey, another ex-champion

Joe knocked out Sharkey in the third round and thereby began another string of victories that led to a championship fight with James J. Braddock the following summer. Again he was tested to the limit when Braddock, cagy veteran that he was, caught him with a right in the first round that put Louis on the canvas. But Louis too had grown in ring wisdom, and this time he was not careless or overconfident. Round by round he punished the old champion, and in the eighth he mercifully put him to sleep with a crackling combination.

Joe Louis had the heavyweight crown, but what did it mean when theatres all over the world were showing slow-motion reruns of the movies of his humiliating knockout by Max Schmeling? The return match was arranged in 1938 at the time when Hitler was at the height of his power in Germany and the United States was beginning to be seriously disturbed by the teachings in his book *Mein Kampf*. His references to "Germany, mistress of the globe by the victorious sword of a master race" helped to inject rival patriotic feelings into this match, with Joe Louis featured as the American representative. Schmeling himself, after hobnobbing with Nazi politicians, talked differently. He now described Joe as "black fellow" and "stupid amateur."

When they met in the ring, however, it was just a matter of seconds before Joe's quick left and his right cross put the boastful Nazi on the canvas. Joe kept his wits, if not his temper, on this occasion, but he seemed to be the only one in the stadium who did. The crowd exploded. When Schmeling rose, blood trickling from his mouth, Joe practically annihilated him. The fight was so short, Schmeling's destruction so complete, that the film of it was used for years afterward against a background of music and announcements to introduce a weekly television program of boxing matches. It was as if it had become a classic example of total victory.

Joe Louis's reign as heavyweight champion of the world was equally glorious. He wore the crown for ten proud years, defended it a total of twenty-five times. That was more times than all the heavyweight champions before him put together had defended the title. He denied no challenger an opportunity. He met them all. If they put up a good fight the first time, as Billy Conn and Jersey Joe Walcott did, he gladly gave them a second chance. In no return match in his career, however, did Louis fail to improve on his first showing. If the challenger went the distance and lost the decision the first time, he was knocked out convincingly the second.

Meanwhile, the simple but sincere, sensitive but unlettered Joe put a number of expressions into the language of sports that have not been forgotten. Joe always seemed to say the right thing—in his own way. When someone predicted that Conn, who was lightning fast on his feet, would stay out of Joe's way, Joe observed, "He can run but he can't hide." When Joe boxed Buddy Baer and turned his purse over to the Navy Relief Fund, a reporter wondered how it felt to be fighting for nothing. Joe told him: "Ain't fighting for nothing. Fighting for my country." During the War Joe predicted that we would win because we were on God's side. That was a point of view that attracted widespread attention. Most people had previously thought that God was on *our* side.

As intuitive as he proved himself to be, however, there was at least one aspect of his tremendous boxing career that even

Joe Louis may not have noted. Before it ended in undefeated retirement, followed later by an unsuccessful return attempt, brought on more by his personal generosity than anything else, Joe Louis had changed the image of the American Negro in the eyes of millions of people around the world. He had also changed the image of the American athlete abroad. And this fact was probably behind a dialogue a reporter heard on the streets of Harlem one day.

"If we had more Negroes like Joe Louis, things would be better for us," one speaker said.

"True," the other answered, "but if we had more white folks like Joe, things would be better still."

SUGAR RAY ROBINSON

[1920–   ]

As SURPRISING as it may seem at first, many of the leading authorities on the manly art, as boxing is sometimes called by sportswriters, have reached the conclusion that while Joe Louis gave us the thrills we remember longest and best and did more than any other athlete in modern times to change the image of the American Negro in the eyes of the world, the greatest all-round fighter the ring has seen in our era, pound for pound, a whole career considered, was not the Brown Bomber or any other heavyweight. He was a boy who at the age of twelve and apparently weighing less than a hundred pounds already looked remarkably stylish as he posed before a camera in a boxer's stance.

Oddly enough, or perhaps not so oddly, the hero this flashy youngster was admiring and trying to pattern himself after was Louis himself. All of this happened, however, before Louis was *Louis* and before Smitty, whose full name was Walker Smith, Jr., became *Sugar Ray Robinson*. It started in Detroit, where both of them grew up, in the slum known as Paradise Valley, in the worst years of the great depression.

Smitty's parents, Leila and Walker Smith, had been married in their home state of Georgia. Soon thereafter they had moved to the Motor City in the hope of finding employment, but things had not gone well in their new home. Handsome Walker Smith, the father, did not succeed in getting anything better than unskilled labor, and the three fine children born to the couple in the three years that followed did not seem to change their father's luck. When it became necessary for the family to accept public relief, the mother's pride was badly hurt. She vowed she would pay it all back. Soon thereafter she found a job of her own with the General Linen Supply Company in Detroit at a salary of eleven dollars a week and promptly notified the relief agency that she no longer needed their aid.

Needless to say, times did not get better immediately. Little Smitty was seven when his parents were divorced, his sisters Evelyn and Marie, eight and nine respectively. But they quickly closed ranks and began working together like a team after the family was broken. Brave, confident Smitty became the seven-year-old man of the family, running errands, washing windows, shining shoes, selling newspapers, scuffling and contending with the swarms of kids on the streets for the few odd jobs the neighborhood afforded. His sisters were equally alert to opportunities to earn money as baby sitters and helpers with household chores. Most important, the girls kept the house in order while their mother was out working.

At the Campbell School, which he attended, and on the street where he spent his afternoons working and playing, Smitty gradually found out what life was like. Indications are that he was an average student in his classes. In games and sports he was ahead of the other kids his age. At ten or eleven he was often chosen to play sandlot ball on teams with boys older than himself. His home influences were such that he never became a toughie, and despite his ability to take care of himself with his fists, when necessary, he was a quiet boy with a soft voice and good manners.

Leila Smith was not blind to the dangers of life on the streets in Paradise Valley in those days. Teen-age gangs were not uncommon. Many of the youngsters of the neighborhood soon found themselves in reform schools. A few came to early violent deaths. Thoughts of this kind may have been in her mind when she began encouraging her son's love for athletic sports. When she agreed, finally, to pay twenty-five cents a month as dues for Junior in the Brewster Community Center, it seemed like a great expense.

In any case, the smiling Junior promptly began to make the most of this wonderful opportunity. In addition to the swimming, the basketball and the other games he liked, he began to show interest in the center's boxing team, first as an observer of the bigger boys already in training for amateur matches, later as the follower and hero-worshiper of the most exciting of all the big boys learning to box at the center at that time, Big Joe Barrow. His own sister Evelyn had gone to school with Joe, and Junior now tagged around after the big guy, watching for opportunities to run errands or do favors for him. Joe, on the other hand, did not fail to respond with the friendliness that seemed to come so natural to him. Sometimes he let young Smitty carry his bag.

Between times Junior began taking a few cracks at the punching bags himself. He would shadowbox, skip rope and otherwise imitate the training routines of the older boys. And he was on hand the night Joe Barrow fought his first amateur opponent. Forgotten by almost everyone except the boy known to his family as Junior, to the crowd around the Brewster Gym as Smitty, is the fact that Joe Louis Barrow was knocked down seven times in that fight while his twelve-year-old hero-worshiper squirmed and suffered and almost broke into tears. After each knockdown, however, the inexperienced Joe got up like a champion and continued to punch, and the very next day he was back at the gym working to correct his mistakes and learn the finer points of boxing.

Junior's young mind put the parts together and learned the lesson along with Joe.

Before he could do much about it, however, the Smith family packed up and moved to New York. They had relatives and friends living there, and some of these had convinced the mother that opportunities for women working as seamstresses were better in New York than in the Motor City. Though she had scarcely enough money for one month's rent after the expense of travel, she had decided to take the risk, and the very next morning she went to work in the big city for the Riverside Laundry and Supply Company at twelve dollars a week. For the next few years, she recalled later, "We lived like gypsies, trying to keep one jump ahead of the landlord."

What she meant, of course, was that twelve dollars a week was simply not enough money to support a family consisting of a mother and three teen-age children, especially when only the mother had a regular job. They moved often in their first years in New York, always hoping to improve their situation.

Meanwhile, Junior made friends with a group of kids who

had hit upon a way to pick up money at night in the vicinity of Times Square. With a tattered harmonica player, a sad-faced drummer and a lonesome urchin with a homemade string instrument providing background music, Junior danced where he could be seen by crowds when they came out to the curb for a breath of air at intermission time. He was a good dancer, a natural-born entertainer, and it was not long before coins were falling in showers around his nimble feet. More than once, above laughter and applause, he heard remarks like, "Gee, this show is better'n the one inside."

When the money was divided, he took his share to his mother to help with the family expenses, but these earnings were not large enough or dependable enough to change anything at home, until one evening a stranger tapped the dancing boy on the shoulder after his performance and offered to put him on the program at the entertainment center called the Palm Gardens. The first night's pay for this was six dollars, and when Junior Smith carried the money home to his delighted mother and sisters, clouds began to disappear miraculously. Life was never quite the same in the Smith household thereafter.

Quick to see the opportunities her children might find in show business, Junior's mother began sending all three of them to the Royal Scotti School of Dancing for lessons that cost a dollar each. To her surprise, however, the talented Junior, whose earnings from dancing had given her the idea in the first place, showed no enthusiasm for the lessons. He missed his appointments, invented excuses for not going and for bringing the money home unused.

His attitude seemed puzzling at first. Was it because dancing came to him so easily, so naturally, he considered the lessons a waste of money? It was hard to know what went on in the mind of a boy like Junior. Later, however, the real reason came to light. In wandering around New York City young Walker Smith had discovered Grupp's Gymnasium and started going there to watch boxers train. Dancing was fine fun in its way. He had a talent for it and enjoyed it, but when he went into a gym where the rattle of small punching bags and the booming of heavy ones made music, when he saw the graceful fighters skipping rope and shadowboxing before big mirrors, smelled the resin dust in the training ring and the sweat and liniment from the dressing rooms, he knew that this was where he belonged. This was his music.

Junior was attending Cooper Junior High at the time, and the story some of his old buddies tell about his next step in boxing took place on West 117th Street. It seems that Junior and a boy named Sonny Leacock stopped to watch some neighborhood kids sparring with boxing gloves before a small crowd of onlookers. Sonny Leacock was well known in that neighborhood. He had been a track star at his school, and he had fought several times in the Police Athletic League. Seeing him there with Junior Smith, whose interest in boxing had also been noticed, gave somebody a notion. How about those two putting on the gloves?

Junior hesitated. Sonny was his friend, and he didn't want to fight his friend. When the kids egged him on, however, and Sonny promptly expressed his willingness, there was nothing Junior could do but accept. The bout lasted about two minutes and ended with Sonny on the ground, his nose bloody, and more and more kids believing the stories Junior had told them about how he had known Joe Louis in Detroit, carried his bag sometimes and even skipped rope and shadowboxed in the gym where the Brown Bomber trained.

Having disposed of a regular Police Athletic League boxer with ease, Junior was ready for PAL bouts of his own, and they were not long in coming. Benny Booksinger, the neighborhood director of this program, began matching him along with other boys who showed promise. At fifteen Junior had the footwork of a professional and the punch of a fighter twice his weight, and the record of his victories soon attracted managers and others interested in promoting amateur boxing. One of them actually called on Mrs. Smith to ask if she would let him manage her son's fighting career.

She did not give him an answer, the whole idea being new, but neither did she disapprove when, a short time later, the PAL director took Junior to the Salem Crescent Athletic Club, where George Gainford was the boxing coach. If Junior's mind was set on becoming a boxer, certainly there was no better place for him to make his start than in a boys' club that met in the basement of a church. The Salem M.E. church on 131st Street and Seventh Avenue was one of Harlem's biggest and best known. Its founder and pastor, the Reverend F. A. Cullen, was a benevolent influence in the whole community. One account that sounds true to people who knew Reverend Cullen personally is that he came upon a bunch of boys shooting craps in a Harlem vestibule and immediately got the idea for the athletic club. He not only reproved the youngsters for wasting their time, but led them to the basement of his church and turned them over to George Gainford. This, according to one story, was the beginning of the

43

Salem Athletic Club, which eventually took in Walker Smith, Jr., and gave him a place on its boxing team.

It was only a matter of weeks before Junior was boxing in an amateur tournament in Grupp's Gym. In a sense this was his debut, and he was terribly anxious to make it good. The boxing he had done before in the PAL was just warm-up, prologue, kid stuff. This was the real thing, an organized amateur event. What was more, his mother and his two sisters were at the ringside to see him. Also on hand were Sonny Leacock and the neighborhood crowd that was now following his activities with interest.

The bright vision of victory, flashing before his young eyes as he came out of the corner to meet his opponent, was a thing of beauty to Walker Smith in that exciting moment. A few seconds later it suddenly disappeared. He had been hit hard, and now he was being belted by gloved fists that seemed to land a dozen at a time. He was not only startled but hurt. One punch caught him so sharply it spun him around, and Junior found himself against the ropes, his back to his opponent, looking down into the hurt, disappointed eyes of his mother.

Ashamed, humiliated, he somehow got himself turned around and into action again. When he regained his senses enough to bob his head and move out of range, he gradually caught the rhythm of the other boxer's movements. The easy spring, the glide he never even had to think about, came back to his legs. All this had happened in half a round. The son of Leila Smith had come out on a cloud, descended to the brink of disaster and then recovered enough to win a second chance. It had been a timeless education. In full control now,

44

he needed only a few moments, a few exploratory jabs, a quick combination, and the rest was up to the referee and the knockdown timekeeper.

All agreed the question of his career was decided, but all were not agreed on at least one important point. Junior wanted to quit school then and there and spend all his time at the gym working with his coach, George Gainford. His mother thought he should stay in school. She asked advice of people in the boxing business, like Dr. Vincent Nardiello, one of the doctors on the boxing commission, and their opinion was the same as hers. His boxing would have to be a part-time afternoon affair till he graduated.

Even so, the Big One, as Junior called Gainford, kept the boy working and learning in the gym and boxing as often as seemed wise for a kid still in Junior High. One night Gainford took some of his young protégés to see the boxing matches in an amateur fight club in Waterbury, Connecticut. In this "amateur" club the boxers were given watches for winning. Often they turned them in for ten or fifteen dollars in cash in the locker room. But the fights were often hotly contested and always worth watching.

The odd thing about the show that night was that one of the principals, a 120-pound boxer, failed to show up. In his dilemma the promoter came to Gainford and asked if he had among his boys one who could fill in at that weight. The Big One looked at Junior. Junior looked at Gainford. Both were thinking the same thing. Junior was ready and willing. The trouble was that Junior did not have an AAU card, as was required of all boys entering that ring. The promoter thought fast. Finally he came up with a plan. He borrowed a card

45

from a young fighter named Raymond Robinson who was present but not fighting that evening.

Under this name and with the card of this boxer Walker Smith, Jr., went into the ring on short notice, scored a quick knockout and returned to New York as *Ray Robinson*. Thereafter he fought all around the amateur circuit under that name, always winning, always improving his style and increasing his power. Back at the same club in Waterbury somewhat later he gave such a remarkable show while putting his opponent to sleep that a sportswriter came over to Gainford afterward and said, "That's a mighty sweet boy you have there, George."

Gainford smiled broadly as he replied, "Sweet as sugar."

That name too stuck to Junior, *Sugar Ray Robinson*.

Ray hit the big time, in amateur ranks, in 1939 when he won the *Daily News* Golden Gloves featherweight championship and then went to Chicago to score an easy victory in the intercity matches. The following year he repeated the same pattern as a lightweight.

In 89 registered amateur fights young Sugar Ray recorded 69 knockouts, 44 of them coming in the first round. In all his amateur bouts, registered and unregistered, a total of 125, he was undefeated.

On October 4, 1940, five months after his twentieth birthday and one week after his final appearance as an amateur, Ray Robinson climbed into the Madison Square Garden ring to fight a four-round preliminary bout on the Henry Armstrong–Fritzie Zivic welterweight championship card. The crowd which was gathering for the main event was, of course, not paying much attention. Even so, the eager, aspiring Ray, with his dancing feet and his ready smile, filled the ring with so much glitter he could not be ignored. His opponent was one Joe Echeverria, and when the bell sent them into action, sparks began to fly immediately. Even at that early date Sugar Ray was a picture boxer. His speed, his rhythm, his coordination, were a treat to the eye. In the second round of his match with Echeverria he measured his man and placed the punch that did the work. Echeverria was counted out on the canvas as the waiting crowd suddenly became attentive and began to take a second look at the lively kid still dancing in the opposite corner.

Ray himself became subdued during the championship fight which followed later. Having showered and had his rubdown, he returned to a ringside seat to watch the fabulous Armstrong attempt to defend his crown. The only boxer ever to win and hold three championships at one time, the stouthearted and ever-willing little battler had pounded out clean victories over featherweight, lightweight and welterweight champions and taken their crowns. While Armstrong's style was as unlike Robinson's as possible, Ray was a great admirer of the fighting heart of Hammering Hank, as were hosts of other fans in 1940, and he pulled for him as he studied the contest which followed. But the tide had turned for Armstrong, and this was the night on which he lost his crown. Nevertheless, Ray made mental notes on the boxer who defeated him and tucked them away for future reference.

Sugar Ray's second professional fight was a carbon copy of the first, except that it occurred in Savannah, Georgia, four days later. His third was a six-round affair at the Bronx Coliseum, and it was a grim test. Facing a hard-hitting and experienced boxer named Mitsos Grispos, Ray had trouble solving his opponent's defense. The rounds wore on, and in the fifth Grispos whipped over a punch that surprised Ray and put him on the canvas, but hard, and in that moment taught the picture fighter a lesson that was even more basic: courage. It took all the will, the heart, the reserve strength and determination Ray could muster to pull himself up and continue the fight. He made it, however, and Ray put on a display in the final round that won him the decision in spite of the knockdown.

He was wiser and more careful in the three other fights he had that year, winning all by knockouts, and in the first half of 1941 he won fourteen times, twelve by KO, two by decision, and became a main-event attraction. On July 21 of that year he was matched with Sammy Angot, the lightweight champion, in a nontitle bout. Despite Ray's exciting six-month record, the champion was heavily favored. Angot was a veteran and wise to all tricks in the ring. Nevertheless Ray knocked him down cleanly in the second round and went on to give the champ a boxing lesson in the rest of the contest.

It was after this fight that leading sportswriters began to search for new words with which to acclaim the prowess of Sugar Ray Robinson. Suddenly they saw him as a little Joe Louis. The boy who so recently had been dancing for nickels before intermission theatre crowds in the Times Square area now found admirers young and old tagging after him as though he were royalty; and if he did not exactly feel like royalty, he certainly began to dress like it. With his lines and his looks, his jaunty walk, he became a kind of fashion plate in his expensive tailoring. Sometimes he was described as the

48

Harlem dandy. Actually, it was just another indication of his flair for the theatre, the stage, show business. No other athlete of our time has made these kinds of public performance seem so closely related as has Sugar Ray Robinson.

After the Angot fight Sugar Ray set his eyes on the welterweight championship, but it proved much more elusive than he had hoped or imagined, and long before he ever won it, he became known across the country as the "uncrowned king" of the welterweights. Champion Fritzie Zivic, one of six fighting brothers, an outstanding boxer by any standard and the conqueror of Henry Armstrong, was the opponent he wanted, and Zivic was probably willing to meet Ray for the crown in late 1941. Unfortunately, however, Zivic lost the title to a relatively unknown fighter a week after Ray defeated Angot. So Ray's pursuit of Zivic that year did not involve the championship.

The two met in New York on the thirty-first of October, after Robinson had added to his Angot win four more decisive ones in August and September of that year. Sugar Ray won the decision by a nod over the capable ex-champion. The fight was close enough and interesting enough to connoisseurs of boxing to create a demand for a return match. This second contest, on January 16, 1942, started like a repeat of the first, but it ended decisively in the tenth round, when Zivic was counted out. Some of those who had followed his career noted that this defeat by Robinson took something out of Zivic that he never regained.

In 1942 Red Cochrane, the welterweight who had removed Zivic's crown, lost an over-the-weight return match to Zivic and promptly joined the Navy, thus freezing the champion-

49

ship for the duration of the war. Sugar Ray carried a draft card too. Meanwhile, however, boxing was booming. Though many boxers, including Joe Louis, were being called into the service, money was plentiful on the home front, and the demand for sports entertainment was great. Every fight meant big money. Robinson set about earning as much of it as he could while waiting for his number to be called.

The year of boxing that started for Sugar Ray with his knockout of Zivic in Madison Square Garden included fourteen fights, eight of them headliners in New York City, two in Philadelphia, and one each in Detroit, Minneapolis, Chicago and Cleveland. Ray won nine by knockouts and five on decisions, one of which was memorable because it marked the beginning of the first of a long series of fights against one of his most rugged opponents, a series that continued for nearly a decade. Jacob La Motta was the opponent, and they met for the first time in the Garden on October 2, 1942.

Sportswriters were calling La Motta the Bronx Bull in grim recognition of his fury, his power, his seeming indestructibility. He made an exciting foe for a fighter who had been a dancer before he became a boxer, whose slenderness and gliding motion offered the greatest possible contrast in styles. While Robinson's speed and skill kept him slightly ahead on points in their first encounter and earned him the judges' decision, the fight was close enough and generated enough tension to call for a return match.

So 1943 like 1942 began with a repeat for Ray, but this time the outcome was different. The buildup too was different. La Motta bellowed for a return match, claiming that Robinson had been lucky to squeeze out the first win and was afraid to come to blows with him again. Ray insisted it was not fear but his desire for more money that made him reluctant to accept a return match. The price had to be right because he was now a big attraction. The effect of the verbal exchange was to build the bout into a grudge match. It was scheduled for the Olympia in Detroit on February 5, and Robinson became a 3–1 favorite by ringtime.

Continually charging forward and slamming away at the slender midsection of his stand-up opponent, La Motta gave Robinson little chance to make use of his classic boxing skills. Ray found himself fighting La Motta's type of toe-to-toe battle, and by the sixth round La Motta seemed the stronger of the two. Meanwhile, however, the crowd was standing practically the whole time, and the nearly deafening roar in the Olympia seldom subsided. In the sixth round the Bronx Bull, driving in close, worked a right to the body and a left hook to the jaw that sent Ray through the ropes and out on the apron of the ring. Hurt and barely able to get to his feet at the count of ten, Ray was saved by the bell.

But he did not cringe, and in the rounds that followed he not only stayed on his feet but fought back with enough reserve power to keep the contest close. When the referee scored the fight 5-4-1 for La Motta, it marked the end of a winning streak for Sugar Ray that had reached a total of 40 professional bouts (32 of them by knockouts) and 125 amateur contests. Even with this loss to La Motta, he had made a record almost unique in the annals of the boxing ring.

Nor had he any cause to be discouraged. La Motta had outweighed him about fifteen and a half pounds for this match, while winning by a margin of one round. The fight itself, moreover, had yielded the largest purse of his career to that time. And now it was Robinson, eager for a chance to redeem the loss and pleasantly receptive to another purse of the same size, who began asking for a return match.

His third encounter with the Bronx Bull was set for just three weeks after the second, and in the same ring. In the meantime, however, Ray received his induction notice from the draft board to report to the Army two days before the fight. Accordingly he was sworn in but given a seven-day furlough to wind up his personal business, which in this case included the La Motta fight. Oddly enough, this bout was another sizzler that bore some resemblance to parts of the second fight. This time La Motta caught Ray with a wicked left hook in the seventh round and put him on the canvas for an eight count. When Robinson got up this time, however, he was poised, calm and confident. For the next three rounds he boxed with style and power, gave his man a boxing lesson, as the expression goes, and won going away. Then on March 1, 1943, the Harlem dandy known as Sugar Ray Robinson, rich and glittering, still hailed as the uncrowned king of the welter-weights, reported at Fort Dix, New Jersey, as private Walker Smith, Jr., of the United States Army.

In the Army, Ray breezed through the basic training and was assigned to the Air Corps at Mitchell Field, Long Island, and given guard detail. Naturally, he attracted attention, with even officers anxious to shake his hand and get his autograph. This assignment was interrupted when Ray suffered an ear infection. Medical examination showed he had a punctured eardrum, which seemed to have been aggravated by gunfire on the training range. Upon leaving Halloran Hospital, after two weeks of treatment, he was transferred to special duty with Casual Detachment Z, then known as the Joe Louis Troupe. Apparently the Army had concluded that the talents of Joe and Ray could be put to a better use than guard duty.

With sparring partners and other necessary personnel they toured Army camps all over the United States, going through their boxing routines to the cheers of soldier audiences. Meanwhile, each of the stars was allowed time off occasionally to fight professionally before civilian fans. Ray engaged in three such bouts after the La Motta fight in 1943 and five more the following year.

La Motta, too, had not been idle. The Bronx Bull had been fighting regularly and improving his reputation. So on February 23, 1945, they renewed their feud. Again Ray made the action lightning fast, La Motta made it furious, and Robinson came off with the decision. But still the issue between them was not settled. They were matched for the fifth time the following September in Chicago, and this time their meeting was out of doors in Comiskey Park with the distance extended to twelve rounds. La Motta, who had made all their clashes hair-raising, figured his greater weight and ruggedness might tell a different story in a longer fight. But the outcome was the same as it had been in three out of the four previous battles, and the relative capacities of the two fighting men overall began to show. Their score seemed finally settled.

Twelve months and sixteen fights later, his Army tour completed, Sugar Ray Robinson, who as a welterweight had long had the prestige of a champion, finally got a chance to make it official by whipping tough Tommy Bell in a hard-fought fifteen-round contest. He fought ten times in his first

53

year as recognized king of the welterweights, putting the crown on the line twice and winning nine bouts by knock-outs, one by decision. In 1948, the second year of his reign, he fought five times, once in defense of the title. He went into battle seventeen times the following year, but all of these were over the weight except the one in Philadelphia against the great and pleasing Kid Gavilan. With the championship at stake, and Sugar Ray performing at his dazzling best, Robin-son handled the almost unbeatable Kid from Cuba as if he owned him

Among the nineteen fights in which Ray engaged in 1950 only one was in defense of his welterweight title. He was fighting more middleweights now, and in that year he won and twice defended the middleweight championship of Penn-sylvania. This in turn led to a match for the middleweight championship of the world. Against whom? The Bronx Bull, Jake La Motta, who had meanwhile won the championship of that division.

So six years after their bitter feud had been interrupted, these veteran gladiators, neither of whom knew what it was to be subdued, met in the Chicago Stadium, February 14, 1951, with the world of television looking on and the diadem they both coveted at stake. At the weighing-in they ex-changed nostalgic remarks.

"Jake, I made you," Ray kidded.

"I done all right for you," the Bull chuckled.

Both were referring to the renown and the riches they had helped the other to win. If a note of gratitude and perhaps fondness could be detected in their words, it did not show in the battle which followed. This one started right where the

54

others had left off. By the fifth round La Motta was feeling good. Pleased with his showing up to then, he charged out of his corner. Pounding with his right and blasting with the dangerous left hook he always carried, he brought blood to Ray's mouth and almost swept him off his feet. Robinson weathered it, and the following round was touch and go. In the seventh, however, Jake seemed to slow down the least bit, and gradually the skillful Ray began to find his mark. Working with utmost care, like an ancient craftsman, he wore his man down in succeeding rounds and ended it in the thirteenth.

It was the high point of a professional boxing career that had already stretched over more than a decade. He had become a perfectionist at his chosen art and posted an amazing record. The following year he fought Joey Maxim for the light heavyweight championship in New York during a heat wave in which the temperature remained above a hundred. Sugar Ray was leading on points when he was overcome by heat prostration between rounds near the end of the fight.

"I wasn't beaten by Maxim," he said afterward. "It was God's will that I finish that way." He retired soon after that fight.

But he did not stay retired, as a boxer in his thirties is entitled to do, as many of his friends and admirers wished he had done; and when he decided to try a comeback, there was at least one great sports columnist who thought he should not be denied. Red Smith wrote on that occasion:

There must have been great figures in sports whom a fellow must regret not having seen—Ketchel, for instance, and Dempsey against Firpo, and Sam Langford; Joe Gans, and Leonard against Tendler; Cy Young and Christy Mathewson and Eddie Collins and

Honus Wagner and Speaker and Cobb at their best; Pudge Heffelfinger and Grange as an undergraduate, and Man O' War.

When the last man who saw Ketchel is gone, there will still be time to talk about Graziano and Zale. It will still be good to remember DiMaggio rounding third and Pepper Martin sliding into second on his face and Stan Musial crouching over the plate. And a fellow will remember Sugar Ray Robinson.

Robinson skipping rope to music, all poetry and rhythm. Robinson punching the face off La Motta. Robinson, wounded and desperate with pride, slugging tough Randy Turpin clear out of the middleweight division.

If Ray wants another payday in the ring, he is entitled to it. If he prefers to take his rest, he earned it. In either event, he will have left us some memories.

Ray decided in favor of the paydays and returned for an almost unbelievable decade of ring warfare against middleweight champions and contenders roughly ten years younger than himself. Bobo Olson, Randy Turpin, Gene Fullmer and Carmine Basilio became his foes in an incredible series in which the once-dazzling mastery of the fading Sugar man reappeared again and again. In a series with Olson reminiscent of the La Motta sequence he improved with each fight till he was handling the capable Bobo with ease. After losing the title to Turpin in England he regained it dramatically at Yankee Stadium in the manner described by Red Smith. He scored a breathtaking knockout over relentless young Gene Fullmer in a return match and then faded to lose the decision in a third. He more than held his own in two title fights with mighty Carmine Basilio.

In his forties, the bounce in his dancing legs almost gone, he still persisted, now gamely, now relentlessly slugging it out, as it were, against time itself.

JACKIE ROBINSON

[1919–   ]

ON JULY 23, 1962, the picturesque village of Cooperstown, New York, turned back the clock to welcome four new members into baseball's Hall of Fame. Fans crowded around a wooden platform on the main street, and nostalgia overflowed, as it so often does in the birthplace of America's national game. Two of those who took their places in the shrine that day were old-timers chosen by the veterans' committee: Edd Roush and Bill McKechnie, sixty-eight and seventy-four years old respectively. The other two were youngsters by comparison. Both Bob Feller and Jackie Robinson were forty-two. Their careers, their heroics, were still fresh in the memories of many, for they had been elected to their places in the famous Hall by baseball writers at the earliest possible date after each had become eligible under the rules.

A few clouds gathered overhead as plaques were presented to the smiling quartet, and each recipient expressed his feelings in a few words. When Jackie Robinson's turn came, he said, "I've been riding on cloud number nine since the election, and I don't think I'll ever come down. Today everything is complete."

When the ceremonies were over, the crowd walked down the wide street to the neat, well-kept ball park called Doubleday Field to witness an exhibition game between the New York Yankees and the Milwaukee Braves on the diamond where this sport had its beginning. Before the game could start, however, thunder ripped the sky, and a tremendous downpour fell on Cooperstown and Doubleday Field. The game had to be canceled.

Perhaps it was just as well. The countryside needed rain desperately. Governor Nelson Rockefeller had already designated the county as a disaster area, as had the U.S. Department of Agriculture. Nothing the Yankees or the Braves could have done that afternoon would have benefited the local people as much as that break in the prolonged drought.

Where the honorees were concerned, the unscheduled conclusion to the day's ceremonies was perhaps just as well too. Certainly an extra hour of calm reflection could not have been considered a hardship to any of them under the circumstances. For Jackie Robinson, however, the road to Cooperstown and the Hall of Fame had been a sports epic of our time, and the strains it had involved were dramatized at that very moment in the streets of Harlem where pickets were carrying signs saying, "Jackie, we like you as a ballplayer, but not as a spokesman for the Negro race."

But two days earlier at a banquet in the Grand Ballroom of the Waldorf Astoria Hotel in New York City a great crowd of his friends who had paid twenty-five dollars a plate for the privilege loudly proclaimed their admiration for this great athlete in both these capacities. Among those present were many of the most distinguished figures in the nation. Their plaudits were loud and long, but some of their feelings were too deep for words. Few men in any sport had ever faced such competitive odds as Jack Roosevelt Robinson faced when he made his bid for a place in organized baseball. With millions of people watching, with a full knowledge of how much depended on him in this calculated bid to break a prevailing color line in the national sport of democratic America, he had accepted the challenge without hesitation. What was there to say about a fellow who had made the grade under conditions like these?

Those who say that great athletes are born, not made, may know what they are talking about, but the extra qualities that Jackie Robinson's double role required came from struggle, hard knocks and hope deferred. He was born the last day of January, 1919, on a sharecropper's farm near Cairo, Georgia. The peonage in which his parents lived with their children at that time was just one step removed from the slavery into which *their* parents and grandparents had been born. Six months after Jackie was born his father deserted the family. This gave the plantation owner an excuse to keep the whole crop the family had raised, instead of the half to which he was entitled, and to evict the widow and her children. Jackie's mother gathered her young ones about her with bitter feelings and found work as a domestic servant. About a year later her brother came to visit.

He had served in the first World War. Afterward he had settled in California. When he returned to visit his people in Georgia, he was dressed so finely they scarcely recognized him. When he heard how things had been with his sister and her children, he was convinced they could do better in California. The troubled mother prayed over her decision. Within a few days she boarded a train with her five children.

They arrived in Pasadena toward the end of May, 1920, and moved into tight quarters with her sister and brother-in-law, her brother, a nephew and her husband's cousin—all crowded into three rooms and a kitchen. There was no hot water, no kitchen sink. Dishes were washed in the same tin tub that served for baths. But Pasadena seemed glorious. There were blue hills on the horizon, and the air was wonderful. Three days later Mrs. Robinson accepted a job doing housework. Meanwhile, the Welfare Department, to which she applied, provided clothing for her and the children.

A young woman of thirty, determined to do the best she could for her children, Mrs. Robinson soon found employment at which she could earn enough money to consider more ample living space for her brood. A house on Pepper Street seemed the answer to her prayers. But a family of Georgia Negroes was not exactly welcome on Pepper Street at that time, and neighborhood irritations became a part of life as the toddler Jackie Robinson first became aware of it.

While the anxious mother lectured her youngsters constantly on proper behavior, their rugged play, their high spirits, their wild speed on skates, for example, drew complaints. By the time he was eight years old, Jackie was doing what came naturally: standing his ground and answering back when the occasion demanded it.

As the Robinson boys became old enough to work, they sought ways to help solve the family's financial problems. Frank and Mack did all kinds of odd jobs, including shining shoes and selling hot dogs. Mack even tried his luck at boxing, but Jackie's first regular employment was carrying the *Los Angeles Times* and the *Los Angeles Examiner* on a regular Sunday morning delivery route. Later he added a Saturday job, helping his uncle tend lawns and shrubbery. By the time he reached adolescence, the first resentment of the neighborhood against the newcomers had pretty well vanished, and Jackie had become a full-fledged participant in the escapades and adventures of the Mexican, Japanese, Negro and Caucasian boys who by then had been welded into the Pepper Street gang. Considering the limitations for wholesome recreation the community placed on some of them, this could have had bad results. Fortunately, the worse trouble the gang got into was arrest for swimming illegally in the city reservoir.

By that time, however, Jackie Robinson was ready for high school, and at Muir Tech it did not take him long to find expression in athletics for the rare coordination and the tightly controlled competitive instinct with which he had been born. If what they saw in him impressed some people as too aggressive or cocky, it certainly did not impress his coaches this way. They were delighted. He was their "holler guy," the team's "sparkplug," a "clutch performer" in their eyes. With Jackie on the teams, Muir Tech became a high school terror in Southern California football, basketball, baseball and track. Every team they faced came into the game under orders to "stop Robinson." One of them finally found a way.

During his senior year Muir Tech played Glendale High School in the Rose Bowl for the conference football championship. On the opening kickoff Jackie made what was for him about an average runback before being tackled and brought down. After the play, as he was getting to his feet, a Glendale player charged into Robinson with enough force to break two of his ribs and force him out of the game. Later Glendale intercepted three passes, all thrown by Jackie's substitute, and turned them into touchdowns. The final score was Glendale 19, Muir Tech 0.

Strange as it may seem in retrospect, the major colleges failed to get steamed up over Jackie Robinson's prospects at this point. When he received no offer of a full scholarship, he decided to enter Pasadena Junior College. Only his oldest brother Frank was upset by this, however. Frank by then had become almost like a father to his youngest brother. He was convinced that nothing but rank injustice was behind this apparent snub. "But we'll show 'em," he vowed. "You just wait till next fall."

But in the practice sessions that fall, Jackie was just a little too anxious to completely fulfill Frank's prophecy. Trying to go outside on a slippery field, he caught his foot in a hole as he cut back, and at that instant two tacklers hit him. He got up limping and finished the game. Later the trainer found that he had broken his ankle. So he was sitting on the bench when the season began. He played quarterback during the last six games that year, however, and the record for these contests was five wins for Pasadena and one scoreless tie. The college scouts who had passed him up in high school were now convinced.

In basketball, baseball and track he made their miscalculation even more emphatic. He got headlines as he starred in each, and in a track meet at Pomona College he set a new world record for the broad jump by a junior college athlete.

Interestingly, the record he broke had been set by his own brother Mack. After Pasadena Junior College had won the baseball championship that year, Jackie was named the most valuable junior college player in Southern California. He had batted .417 and stolen twenty-five bases in twenty-four games. Jimmy Dykes, manager of the Chicago White Sox at the time, was quoted in a newspaper as saying, "That boy could play major league baseball at a moment's notice."

During the football season of his second year at Pasadena JC the name of Jackie Robinson became something of a legend in Southern California. People who spoke about UCLA or USC had to be careful or they would find themselves interrupted by someone who would insist that the only football player worth mentioning at that moment was "that colored boy out at Pasadena." By the end of the season they were pointing to the statistics. Jackie had led his team to eleven straight victories and the junior college championship. He had scored 131 points and gained over 1,000 yards from scrimmage, and he had indeed been the sparkplug of a team some local fans ardently remember as "the best football team ever assembled at a junior college."

San Francisco sportswriters were skeptical of all this Jackie Robinson buildup when the Pasadena team came into Kezar Stadium on November 11 to play San Francisco Junior College. But his seventy-five-yard touchdown run the first time he carried the ball was convincing. He left the field three quarters later to an astonishing ovation.

After Pasadena, of course, he had a wide choice of senior colleges. One of the main reasons he chose UCLA was his brother Frank. The idea of Jackie's playing at a college so far away from home that Frank could not attend the games was unthinkable to either of them. But Frank never saw Jackie play at UCLA. He died in a motorcycle accident in May of 1939. As a result Jackie's brilliant years as a Bruin star were tinged with inner sadness.

The memory of Frank, the oldest of the three Robinson boys, zooming around Southern California on his motorcycle, hurrying to be on hand to shout encouragement from the sidelines to the younger brother to whom he was devoted and to whose successful future he now transferred all his own aspirations and faded hopes, was with Jackie constantly that fall in the UCLA backfield. During the basketball season, when he averaged twelve points a game, and the following spring when the track season began and he broad jumped twenty-five feet six inches, he was still hurt by the loss of the brother who had been like a father to him. But in his second year as a Bruin he had inspiration of another sort. By then he had met and become interested in a coed named Rachel Isum.

But Jackie's was not the only star that glittered for the Bruins in football in 1939. Indeed, despite Jackie's twelve yards per carry that season, it was his Touchdown Twin who made All-American. Kenny Washington, also a Negro, was a halfback big and powerful enough to play tackle on any team. At Lincoln High, where his remarkable career began, he had been hailed as a Paul Bunyan of football. A mighty runner and a dependable passer, he was just what was needed to loosen up the defense for Jackie's broken field heroics. Together they were fabulous, and with them as headliners their team drew tremendous crowds to the Los Angeles Colosseum. Nor was the right end on that team a player who

64

JOE LOUIS

United Press International Photo

SUGAR RAY ROBINSON

JACKIE ROBINSON

LEROY (SATCHEL) PAIGE

WILLIE MAYS

JESSE OWENS

WILTON NORMAN CHAMBERLAIN

JAMES NATHANIEL BROWN

ALTHEA GIBSON

could be overlooked. He was Woodrow Wilson Strode, himself a candidate for All-American, later a successful motion picture actor in roles that highlighted his bronze physique, his sculptured features. Jackie's main competition in basketball that season came from across town, where Ralph Vaughn, the USC wizard, was making history.

The following year, with Washington and other key players gone, the football bubble seemed to burst for UCLA. They won only one game, but in that one Jackie Robinson was his old exciting self, scoring on sixty- and seventy-five-yard runs.

When he decided in the spring of 1941 to drop out of college before graduating, the Los Angeles sportswriters and editors showered him with rare praise. George T. Davis, of the *Herald Express*, declared, "It's my honest opinion that Jackie Robinson will go down in history as the greatest all-around athlete in Pacific Coast history." He was less well-known in the East, however, and in August when he went to Chicago to practice with the College All-Stars, there was little excitement until the sportswriters there saw him. One look convinced them. According to the United Press, "It took one scrimmage to establish the Negro boy's rightful place among the All-Stars." The All-Stars, of course, were outclassed by the professional Bears in the game itself, but they managed to score two touchdowns, and one of them was by Jackie.

That fall Robinson played professional football with the Honolulu Bears in Hawaii. On December 5, the season over, he boarded the steamer *Lurline* for home. It was two days out when the Japanese attacked Pearl Harbor on December 7, and the ship had to sail blacked out at night from then on.

Drafted into the Army as he reached home, he applied for Officer Candidate School. At Fort Riley in Oklahoma, where he was stationed, Negroes had not thus far been accepted for OCS, and Jackie confronted for the first time as an adult the problem of racial discrimination. His reaction was automatic. He resented it. Joe Louis, who was still heavyweight champion though serving in the Army, happened to be assigned to Fort Riley for a few days at that time. Jackie met Joe and told him how angry it had made him to discover that Jim Crow was going to prevent him from attending OCS. In his calm, unexcited way Joe went to a telephone and called by long distance a friend who was employed as an adviser to the Secretary of Defense. The friend flew out to Riley immediately and checked the complaint. Within a few days Jackie Robinson and several other Negroes were in OCS.

Jackie received his commission and served as a morale officer. After his discharge he accepted a coaching job at Sam Houston College in Texas, but this was cut short when he received a letter offering him three hundred dollars a month to play baseball for the Kansas City Monarchs, a Negro team. He would not move for that amount, but he demanded and got four hundred dollars and joined the Monarchs in training camp at Houston in April of 1945. He had been working out with them only a few days, however, when he received a telephone call from Wendell Smith, sports editor for *The Pittsburgh Courier*, a Negro weekly, saying that the Boston Red Sox of the American League had agreed to give tryouts to a few Negroes and asking Jackie to come up. Jackie hesitated, doubting the sincerity of the offer, but he let himself be talked into taking the trip.

66

To Jackie Robinson, Sam Jethroe and Marvin Williams, the players who went to Boston with Smith for this so-called tryout, the whole experience turned out to be something of a laugh. Nothing came of it. So far as they could see, nothing was ever intended to come of it. Actually, however, it was not wholly without significance. Something had been started. A small fire was burning unseen. Writers like Ed Sullivan and Damon Runyon and others less well-known were putting heat under baseball's bosses. The recent war against Hitler had changed the racial attitudes of many Americans. Joe Louis's appealing image had had an effect. How could baseball continue as the American pastime while practicing a policy of Jim Crow that contradicted the principles of democracy? Discussions like this and "tryouts" like the one in Boston continued.

While it went on, at least one man was giving serious thought to ways and means of overcoming the difficulties and bringing about a change. He was Branch Rickey, owner of the Brooklyn Dodgers. He had gone to school with Negroes in Ohio in his boyhood, and he had coached Negro college students at Ohio Wesleyan. His own thoughts on the subject were clear. The apparently farcical Red Sox tryout had not escaped his notice. He made a mental note of one name: Jackie Robinson. Eventually he added other names to his little private list: Don Newcombe, Roy Campanella. But he was not ready to disclose his plans. He went ahead quietly checking out prospects and assuring himself of the complete backing of the Dodgers' directors and stockholders. His number one aim, of course, was to strengthen the Dodger ball club. His number two aim was to help lift the cloud that hung over the national sport.

Success in each would depend to a large extent on the player himself. His ability as a player had to be beyond question. He would have to make the grade in everybody's book. Important as this was, however, his poise, his coolness under fire, was even more vital. He would have to be a real man out there on the field. He could not afford to give ground. Neither could he afford at any time to let his feelings boil over. When the brush-back came at the plate, when spikes were in the air at second or third, when insults came from the stands, whenever there were tense situations and feelings went high, he would have to be in control of himself.

When Rickey indicated that he had settled on Robinson as his pioneer, there were those who seriously questioned Jackie's habit of arguing and standing his ground. They favored a more submissive type of player. Rickey decided otherwise, however, and Robinson was hired on October 23, 1945, and sent to the Montreal Royals as tension mounted across the nation.

Could Jackie Robinson succeed under such pressure? Could any athlete do it? No precedent existed. The triumphs of Joe Louis and Jesse Owens were still vividly remembered, but theirs were individual accomplishments. Jackie Robinson was asked to make good with teammates, coaches and a manager who had been conditioned by attitudes of prejudice, many of them brought up from the Deep South. He was called on to win the respect of fans who could not be expected to be more emancipated than these. Then there was the vast public at home that followed baseball results in newspapers and on the air. The opposing teams, the enemies on the field of play, who should have been the sole concern of the aspiring athlete, were actually the least of Jackie's worries.

There were 25,000 people on hand to see Jackie when he appeared for the first time in organized baseball. It happened in Jersey City on the eighteenth of April, 1946. To say that Robinson was the center of attention is an understatement. Every spectator in the stands was there to see the debut of the Montreal second baseman. When he went to bat the first time, they held their breath, and he grounded out to the infield. In his second time at bat he drove in three Montreal runs as he lined a 335-foot home run over the left-field wall with two men on base. But that was just the beginning. In three more times at bat that day Jackie beat out two bunts and put a whistling single into right field for a total of four hits in five attempts. For good measure, he stole two bases and so unnerved the Jersey City pitcher he committed a balk that forced Jackie home with a run. Robinson went on to win the International League batting championship with an average of .349 and to lead the league in fielding with a .985 average. He stole forty bases that season.

His season with the Royals was epitomized in the Little World Series of 1946, when his team met the Louisville Colonels for the minor league championship. The games played in Louisville were tense almost to the point of anguish for all concerned, and the fact that the local club owners had put a quota on the number of Negro fans who could attend had intensified rather than reduced the tension. The series was nip and tuck all the way, but when Jackie emerged the hero in the final and decisive game, joy overflowed in Montreal, and Robinson had to be protected from his admirers. According to sportswriter Sam Martin, "It was probably the only day in history that a black man ran from a white mob with love instead of lynching on its mind."

Jackie came up to the Dodgers of the National League the following year as a first baseman. The Dodgers won the pennant that season, as they did in five of the next ten years in which Jackie Robinson played on the team. In the majors as in the minors he was Rookie of the Year in his first season. Two years later he was named the National League's Most Valuable Player. During his ten years in the majors Jackie stole 197 bases, more than any other player for a similar period. He was selected to play in six All-Star games. He led National League second basemen in fielding four times. He set a National League record for double plays by a second baseman in 1951 with 137. He set a National League fielding record for a second baseman the same year with an average of .992. His overall batting average in organized baseball was .311.

In January 1957 Jackie decided it was time for him to ring down the curtain on athletics. In an article in *Look* magazine he wrote, "I've made my living in baseball for the past twelve years. Now, I'm quitting the game for good. There shouldn't be any mystery about my reasons. I'm 38 years old, with a family to support. I've got to think of my future and our security. At my age, a man doesn't have much future in baseball—and very little security. It's as simple as that."

He wrote his statement on the stationery of the Chock Full O' Nuts Company, the snack bar chain which he had just joined as vice president and personnel director. He was still serving ably in this capacity and making his influence felt widely as a citizen and a leader when, five years later, he received notice of his election to baseball's Hall of Fame.

LEROY (SATCHEL) PAIGE

[1906–   ]

L OOKING AT IT in another way, a good many people have
thought that it would have been more just if LeRoy Robert
Paige, instead of Jackie Robinson, had been the first Negro to
break into the big leagues. Even if he had, however, Jackie
probably would have beat him to baseball's Hall of Fame.
The rules do not permit one to be named to this shrine for at
least five years after retirement from the game, and Old Satch,
as he is fondly known, was still out there throwing long after
Jackie hung up his spiked shoes. While Jackie was going up to
Cooperstown for the Hall of Fame ceremonies, in fact, the
legendary Satchel Paige was clicking his false teeth, smiling
mysteriously and declaring, "Maybe I'll pitch forever."

Any photograph of this quaint genius as he performed his
magic in the American League between 1948 and 1954 might
be entitled "A Man and His Memories." In his heyday in
organized baseball Paige could look back on nearly thirty
years of almost unbelievable pitching. A modest estimate of
the number of games in which he had gone to the mound was
2,500 and 2,000 was conservative for his victories. The fact

that many of these games were in a sense "unofficial" did not mean that Satch had not pitched gloriously, and the accounts of his prowess were not just hearsay. Players like Dizzy Dean, Bob Feller and Joe DiMaggio saw and played against him in those days and never afterward seemed able to find adjectives big enough to describe his talents. Under the circumstances the wise but humorous twinkle in his old eyes, the faint, enigmatic smile, were understandable. Old Satch had been around, and it was no longer a secret.

When he finally walked out of a quarter of a century of dim sideshow baseball into the bright sunshine of the big leagues, 20,000 fans at Cleveland Stadium rose for ten minutes of unbroken roaring, as one spectator put it. This gave the old fellow a cozy, at home feeling. He had a wonderful understanding of people in crowds, especially those who had paid money to come out to see him pitch. He liked them. He seemed always in personal communication with them, and the afternoon of July 7, 1948, in Cleveland Stadium was no exception, except when one remembered how old he was, how long he had waited, how far he had traveled to reach this point. Remembering these things, the ovation was enough to bring tears to ordinary eyes but not enough to keep Paige from responding graciously in the way in which he was accustomed. He gave them two scoreless innings in relief. He went on from there to give the Cleveland Indians and Bill Veeck, their owner who had given him this chance in the twilight of his long career, six important victories against one defeat in the home stretch of that season. His earned run average was 2.47. He had forty-five strikeouts. When baseball writers suggested naming him Rookie of the Year, Satch

72

asked wryly, "Which year?"

The same question has been asked by others with respect to the date of Paige's birth. His mother, who was nearly ninety at the time, put the year at 1903 and mentioned an old Bible as the authority. To this Satch answered, "What mama knows when her little child was born?" His own date was 1906, and he claimed that there was a birth certificate in Mobile for a LeRoy Page on July 7 of that year. He explained away the difference in the spelling of the last name. A researcher who wrote a magazine article on Paige in 1948 referred to a World War II draft registration and said that the date was in September of 1904. Which year, indeed!

In any case, there seems to be agreement that the place was Mobile, Alabama. LeRoy was the seventh of eleven children crowded into the four-room "shotgun" house (one room behind the other) they called home. The father was a gardener, the mother a washerwoman, but together they seldom earned enough to satisfy the family's basic needs. Neither seemed to care very much when LeRoy started missing school more than he attended. They were more interested in the pennies he brought home after selling bottles picked up in alleys. LeRoy, however, soon found a way to increase his earnings.

Nearly six feet tall at the age of twelve, he began carrying bags at the Mobile railroad station. For these services he received ten cents per bag, and by rigging up a stick and rope on which he could hang half a dozen or more bags at a time, he made it pay even better. Someone who saw him staggering along under his load one day, looking for all the world like a tree of satchels, gave him the name that he has since made famous.

Meanwhile, however, picking up empty bottles and helping to sweep the stands at the Eureka Gardens, a semipro baseball park, he caught his first glimpse of a game he had little hope of actually playing. Not owning a baseball, he began entertaining himself by throwing rocks. To his surprise he discovered that he could hit targets others thought almost impossible. When his mother sent him to the yard to catch and kill a chicken for her, he did it with a rock. He discovered also that he could kill flying birds with rocks. With an arm like this it was only a step to becoming pitcher for the baseball team of the W. H. Council School.

It was also, unfortunately, just a step to becoming a sort of sniper with rocks for the kids of his street in their battles with enemies from other neighborhoods. Before long Satch was having trouble with the police as well as truant officers. Then one day, his pockets stuffed with cheap but bright and shiny stuff in a downtown store, a towering white man suddenly took him by the shoulder and carried him to police headquarters. The next day the following entry appeared in the books of the county courthouse in Mobile:

"On this day, the twenty-fourth of July, 1918, LeRoy Paige is ordered committed to the Industrial School for Negro Children at Mount Meigs, Alabama."

His mother screamed, "Not for just that little bit of junk!" But it didn't do any good. He was twelve when he went to the reform school. He was going on eighteen when he returned. Automatically he wandered over to the Eureka Gardens where the semiprofessional Negro team called the Mobile Tigers still played. Soon he was on the mound pitching for them.

Paige's pitching was a delight to watch from the start. There seemed to be humor in it because of his slow walk, the way he hesitated, raising his foot high in the air before coming down with the blazing speed that was certainly no joke. He calculates he must have won thirty games that year as a semi-pro and lost one. Though they paid him off mainly in lemonade, he was still giving the Mobile fans chuckles and thrills when, one day in 1926, Alex Herman, owner of the Chattanooga Black Lookouts in the old Negro Southern League, offered him "steady money with a league team." Apparently the skinny pitcher, six feet three inches tall and weighing just 140 pounds, needed the permission of his mother before leaving home, but she gave it when Herman promised to watch out for the boy like a father and to send his fifty-dollar-a-month salary home to her.

The trail of Satchel Paige's baseball wanderings grows somewhat dim at this point. Indeed, his odyssey is in itself a kind of history of Negro baseball teams in the United States prior to the breakthrough into the regular ranks of the national game.

Negro baseball became organized for the first time in 1920 with the founding at Kansas City, Missouri, of the Negro National League. A year later an Eastern League was set up. In 1924 the two organizations began playing their own World Series, and the relationship continued until the depression years. Nevertheless detailed records were not always retained. Evidence has been found to substantiate Paige's pitching for the Black Lookouts of Chattanooga, for the Black Barons of Birmingham in 1928 and later for the Baltimore Black Sox, the Chicago American Giants and the Pittsburgh

Crawfords. He remained with the latter for seven years. In 1933 his record with the Crawfords was thirty-one games won and four lost in a total of forty-two games pitched. At one time he had a winning streak of twenty-one consecutive games and sixty-two scoreless innings.

With accomplishments such as these in the records, perhaps it is not surprising that some of his more amazed fans began creating legends in those days. His strikeout victims complained that his fast ball tended to disappear as it approached the plate. To this a spectator added, "*Disappear* is the word. I've heard about Satchel throwing pitches that wasn't hit but that never showed up in the catcher's mitt. They say the catcher, the umpire and the bat boys looked all over for that ball, but it was gone. Now how do you account for that?"

More responsible observers have insisted, however, that the Pittsburgh Crawfords were easily the greatest team in the world at one time while Paige was with them and that they "might have won pennants in either major league." In addition to Paige they had a catcher named Josh Gibson whose reputation as a hitter was comparable to Paige's as a pitcher. With these two the Crawfords were invincible.

Pitching for a Bismarck, North Dakota, team in 1934, Paige appears to have had another fabulous season. After it was over, he pitched against Dizzy Dean in an exhibition game which lasted thirteen innings. Paige's team won, 1–0, but the significant thing about the contest was the presence in the stands of a spectator named Bill Veeck, the man who eventually brought Satchel into the big leagues. Veeck's comment on this occasion was, "It's the best I've ever seen."

Soon thereafter, however, Paige and Josh Gibson and other

Negro stars from the United States signed with the Dominican Republic to play winter baseball on that Caribbean island. It marked the beginning of a series of such winters thereafter for Paige with teams in Venezuela, Mexico, Cuba, Puerto Rico, Colombia and elsewhere in Latin America.

Meanwhile, he spent summers in the United States pitching for such teams as the Homestead, Pennsylvania, Grays, and the Kansas City Monarchs and playing exhibition contests. During this period he is said to have received five hundred dollars for every game in which he appeared. In one of these in California in 1937 he was praised by Joe DiMaggio as "the best pitcher he had ever faced."

The following year, pitching in Mexico City and at the peak of his skill and fame, Paige reared back to throw a simple sidearm curve and felt something snap. It hurt so badly he could scarcely lift his arm. When the doctor examined him back in Kansas City, he got the bad news. According to the specialist, old Satch was through, definitely through.

Paige would have been disconsolate if he could have just believed his ears, but he simply could not conceive of his dependable right arm betraying him in this way. Surely the arm that had lifted him from poverty and delinquency in Mobile, that had withstood zero weather in Canada and burning desert heat, that had never balked after all-night bus rides nor acted up as a result of overwork or bad food or cheap rooming houses, wouldn't do that to him now. He recalled the four Negro World Series and East-West All-Star games in which the old soup bone had served him without the slightest complaint, sometimes before crowds of 50,000 and more. Had it been an arm of a different color, folks were saying in

77

1938, major league club owners might have paid up to $150,000 for its services.

As hard as it was for Satch to believe it, he was nevertheless unable to lift his arm, and within a month he was unemployed. The Monarchs took pity on him and made him a coach. During the next year he traveled with the second team in this capacity. It was a miserable season. Time dragged painfully. Some fourteen months later, at the age of about thirty-five, he was so deep in the dumps he was ready to quit baseball when one afternoon a queer thing happened. Someone overthrew first base during the pregame warm-up and old Satch shuffled over, picked the ball up and threw it back to the pitcher. It was just about the simplest thing one could do in a ball park, but it caught the eyes of the whole Monarch team and no one moved or spoke for a moment.

Satch, too, was mystified for an instant, but he recovered before the others. Walking slowly to the dugout, Paige picked up a glove and called for a ball. Without saying a word, the Monarchs' catcher left his place behind the plate and planted himself about the correct pitching distance away from Satch. Then old Satch began to throw, easily at first, then harder and harder. Still nobody moved or spoke, not even in the grandstands. The catcher made motions with his hands and tried to get the old fellow to take it easy, but Satch continued to fire away. Then suddenly he stopped and looked around.

"Well," he announced, his eyes bright. "I'm back."

The news went around in a hurry. Old Satch was back. He helped pitch the Monarchs to victory in the Negro World Series of 1942. Four years later he was credited with helping the Monarchs to win another pennant, "allowing only two runs in ninety-three innings and running a streak of scoreless innings to sixty-four," according to *The New York Times*. By then Paige had pitched a number of no-hit and one-hit games and tied Bob Feller's record in striking out eighteen batters in a single game.

Satch had, of course, seen his best years by 1946, when the employment of Jackie Robinson by the Brooklyn Dodgers broke down the color barrier in the major leagues. His fast ball was not what it had been, and there was little interest in bringing the aging hurler into the big time. In the fall of the next year, however, Satch outpitched Bob Feller of the Cleveland Indians in an exhibition game in Los Angeles, winning 8–0 and striking out sixteen Cleveland batters. This made such an impression on Bill Veeck, owner of the Indians, whose interest in Paige dated back to the game Satch had pitched against Dizzy Dean a decade earlier, that he decided to offer Paige a contract.

The following season, 1949, Paige was troubled with a stomach disorder, and his record was spotty. Moreover, Veeck sold his interest in the Indians that year, and in February 1950 the new owners gave Paige his release. In doing so, General Manager Hank Greenberg was quoted as saying, "He did the job asked of him in bringing up six victories toward the pennant in 1948. We want to release him now so he can make his own plans for the 1950 season."

Released from Cleveland, Paige returned to the Kansas City Monarchs. According to the magazine *Baseball* he "pitched 62 games around the nation in 1950 and was on the same type of extensive junket . . . when Veeck re-entered big league baseball with the Browns." Paige's stomach disorder had meanwhile responded to treatment, and when Veeck bought the St. Louis American League team, he promptly called the amazing old hurler back to the majors as a relief pitcher. That was in July. In the rest of the 1951 season Paige went to the mound twenty-three times for the Browns, but the team was weak, and his record was three wins and four losses. The next year the Browns were stronger, and Paige's record with them in relief was better. He remained with the Browns till the club was sold and the new owners were given permission by the American League to move the team to Baltimore.

So it was back to the minor leagues again in 1955. Six years later he was still taking his turn on the mound. By then he had begun to wonder seriously if this might not go on forever.

WILLIE MAYS

[1931–   ]

"Say hey!"

With this happy expression on his lips a boy of nineteen bounced out of the Polo Grounds dugout, trotted to his position in center field and got his first glimpse of a New York baseball crowd in the bleachers, boxes and grandstand seats. To say he played as if he enjoyed the game is too mild. He played as if he had invented it. There was seldom a day on which he did not do something extraordinary on the field: an "impossible" running catch, an "unbelievable" home run out of the park, a daring adventure on the base paths, a spine-tingling throw from the outfield to home plate. All were alike to the amazing Willie Mays. All seemed to bring the same chuckles of delight from the boy who loved to play, whose heart was a leaf.

By the summer of 1954 sportswriters had almost run out of words to describe the impression Willie made on them, but *Time* summed it up when it put under his picture, "A boy's glee, a pro's sureness, a champion's flair." Willie had just returned from the Army after two years of service, and the good news was that he was the same Willie the fans remembered. In fact, he seemed better than ever.

The group with which he traveled to Cleveland for the All-Star Game that year included Charley Grimm, one of the National League coaches, and it was Grimm who remarked after the trip, "Mays is the only ballplayer I ever saw who could help a club just by riding on the bus with it." What he had in mind, of course, was Willie's bubbling humor, his spirit and the inspiration he gave to his teammates. But if this was one of the things that an experienced coach noticed, there was much more that anybody could see and appreciate.

Willie Mays, as his autobiography says, was *Born To Play Ball*. Both his parents were athletic. His father worked in one of the steel mills near Birmingham, Alabama, but he was best known around the plant as an outfielder for the mill's baseball team. He was nicknamed "Kitty Cat" because of the way he moved and handled himself on the field, and he too was the son of a baseball player. Walter Mays, Willie's grandfather, was still remembered in Tuscaloosa, Alabama, for his pitching on amateur teams around the turn of the century. Willie's mother was a high school track star in her girlhood.

Born on May 6, 1931, in the steel town of Westfield, thirteen miles out of Birmingham, Willie got his baseball talents honestly, as the saying goes. However, the marriage that produced them did not last long. Willie's parents were divorced when he was about two. When his mother remarried, he was taken to live with his Aunt Sarah, the wife of his father's brother. His father remained single but took his meals at Aunt Sarah's, and this was how the baseball talk between father and son began. After supper in the evenings Kitty Cat would fill the mind of his youngster with everything he could tell about the wonderful game. When Willie was older, Kitty Cat took him to the ball field to watch the games played by the company team. Soon the two were playing a pepper game together in the evenings, and Willie was finding sandlot games in which he could play in the afternoons.

At school, however, Willie discovered other games he liked just as well. Football attracted him before he finished grammar school, and one day when he was thirteen, he climbed a tree to watch a game between Fairfield Industrial High and West View High. He became so absorbed in the game, so excited, so thrilled, he forgot where he was. He threw up his hands to cheer, fell out of the tree and broke his arm. It was his first sports injury.

When he became a student at Fairfield Industrial, a year or so later, he went out for football and showed talent as a passer. He took up basketball about the same time, and in his sixteenth year he was the high scorer of the county in this sport. The only reason he did not play baseball at Fairfield was that Fairfield Industrial did not have a baseball team, but Willie made up for it by playing summers with teams around the neighborhood and in nearby communities.

Willie usually pitched in these games, and he has recalled a day when he was fourteen and went nine innings under Alabama's broiling summer sun. Rounding third base, after hitting a long one that had to be stretched to a homer in order to win the game for his team, Willie felt his head begin to swim. He swooned as he touched home plate and had to be carried off the field by Kitty Cat, who had been among the spectators. In the future Willie would have to be careful not to let his boundless energy cause him to overexert himself, the father advised. Come to think about it, he might do well to let somebody else do the pitching. Someone who knew how to ease up and sort of pace himself.

Willie listened to his father and took his advice. From then on he always played the outfield, and before he was out of high school, Kitty Cat introduced him to a man named Piper Davis, manager of the Birmingham Barons, one of the best teams in the Negro National League. Kitty Cat was still playing ball himself at the time, and Piper Davis decided that if young Willie was anything like a chip off the old block, it might not be a waste of time to give him a tryout. He agreed to take him on as a utility player for the summer.

When an injury to the regular center fielder gave Willie a chance to play, he did so well he could not be moved. Meanwhile, Kitty Cat watched his boy with a father's pride. As soon as he was sure that Willie had definitely won the center field position with the Barons, the old Cat's eyes brightened and he decided to hang up his spikes. Talking about it several years later, he recalled, "I didn't see any use of playing any longer after the boy went with the Barons. That was when I knew for sure Willie was going to be a great player."

Within weeks Willie caught the eye of a major league scout. It was on a night in June of 1949, and the Birmingham Black Barons were playing the Memphis Red Sox. The scout was Bill Maughn of the Boston (later Milwaukee) Braves. He soon learned from Thomas Hayes, a Negro undertaker of Memphis, who owned the Black Barons, that Willie could not be signed while still a high school student. Still there was the question in Maughn's mind as to whether the rule against signing high school boys applied in Willie's case, since Willie

84

had already turned professional and was playing baseball for money in an organized league. Happy Chandler, then the baseball commissioner, ruled that it did.

During the year that followed, while Willie completed high school and continued to play with the Barons, Maughn did not succeed in transferring his own enthusiasm for the youngster to the owners of his own team, so he passed the tip along to Eddie Montague, a Giant scout. Actually, the Giant scouts had a chance to see Willie play in the Polo Grounds early in May of 1950, but they were so busy watching another player in whom they were interested they scarcely noticed Willie. It was when Montague, still following this other player around, saw Willie playing in Birmingham a week or so later that he got the shock of his baseball life.

"My eyes almost popped out of my head during batting practice when I saw a young Negro boy swing the bat with great speed and power. His hands had the quickness of a young Joe Louis throwing punches. I also saw his great arms. During the game, his speed and fielding ability showed up. This was the greatest ballplayer I had ever seen in my life."

Montague went to his hotel that night and phoned these impressions to his home office. Just a day or two later, at Willie's home in Fairfield, with Aunt Sarah and Kitty Cat and Willie's young sister looking on and approving, the Say Hey kid put his signature on a contract that made him the baseball property of the New York Giants, and Montague rushed out and sent it to his home office by air-mail special. Though it appeared that Willie had no contract with the owner of the Black Barons, and hence believed himself to be a free agent in this matter, Giant officials took the position that it was no more than right to make a payment to Thomas Hayes. They sent him a check for $10,000.

The Giants sent Willie to Trenton, New Jersey, where they operated a farm team in the Interstate League. Playing with Trenton that summer, Willie batted .353, got surprising distance on many of his hits and repeatedly made circus catches in the outfield. Long before the 1950 season ended, it was plain that the Interstate League wouldn't be able to hold him long. The following year he moved up to the Minneapolis Millers of the American Association.

Meanwhile, Leo Durocher, the Giant manager, watched Willie working out in spring training down in Florida, and what he saw could be described as an eyeful. Willie was doing all the amazing things he loved to do on a baseball diamond, and as usual he was having big fun while doing them. Durocher liked what he saw, and he did not forget it when Willie left with the Millers.

Willie played thirty-five games with Minneapolis as the 1951 season began, ran his batting average up to .477, including eight home runs, and scored thirty-eight runs. The Giants, meanwhile, started the season with a losing streak of eleven games. Putting two and two together, Durocher decided to make a move. He went to the telephone and called Minneapolis. He got Willie's number, but Willie was not in, and nobody seemed to know where he was. They found him eventually—at the movies, eating popcorn and enjoying the picture.

"The manager of the theatre came out on the stage and said for me to get in touch with manager Tommy Heath of the Millers at the hotel," Mays recalled later.

Heath was waiting to congratulate Willie on being called up by the Giants so soon, but to his surprise, Willie was not overjoyed by the news. Maybe he was still a little annoyed at being called out of a movie he liked, but he asked Heath to call Durocher in New York and tell him Willie was not coming.

"What do you mean, you're not coming up?" Lippy Leo barked into the telephone when Heath finally put Willie on.

"I can't play that kind of ball," Willie protested.

It took Durocher about sixty seconds to win that argument, and in a matter of hours Willie Mays was headed east to join the Giants in Philadelphia. He reported at Shibe Park on May 25, 1951.

In five times at bat that day, however, Mays failed to get a hit. He also failed to get a hit the next day in Philadelphia. And the next, though the Giants won all three. He couldn't remember going that long without a hit since his first week with Trenton when he made outs the first twenty-two times at bat before solving Interstate League pitching. But he had shaken that slump eventually, and perhaps he could do it again. His first at-bat with the Giants in the Polo Grounds was his twelfth at-bat in the major leagues, and in this game the Giants were playing the Boston Braves, with Warren Spahn pitching. After those three games in Philadelphia Willie Mays had reason to be tight and overanxious. Spahn greeted him with a blazing fast ball.

Willie's bat met it solidly. All the announcer said on the radio was, "G'bye!" The ball went out of the park. So Willie's first major league hit was a homer off one of the greatest pitchers of all time, and it would be pleasant to say that this

87

ended his long hitless streak, but it did not. After that homer he started another string of goose eggs which eventually showed one hit in twenty-six times at bat. After that, however, he got nine hits in his next twenty-four times up, and the slump was soon forgotten.

The players on the team kidded him. He kidded back, and the Giants, who had been in fifth place when he joined them, began to win games and to improve their standing in the National League. They started a win streak which continued until it reached sixteen games without a defeat, and this was doubly interesting, because it had been just sixteen years since any other National League team had won that many games in a row. Indeed, the story of how the New York Giants caught the league-leading Brooklyn Dodgers in 1951 in a spine-tingling home stretch and won the pennant from them in a breathtaking play-off series of three games is still a high spot in the history of this exciting and colorful sport.

Willie Mays batted well during that drive by the Giants to one of their most unforgettable pennants, but he fielded even better, and at least one of the plays he made in a crucial game, with everything hanging on it, has taken its place in baseball lore as a classic. The Giants were playing the Dodgers, and the score was 1–1 in the top of the eighth inning. At bat was the dangerous Dodger hitter Carl Furillo. On third was a fast base runner named Billy Cox. Furillo connected, his drive whistling toward right center, and Willie took off from his position in dead center. This meant he was traveling in the wrong direction for a throw, but a throw was absolutely necessary to keep Cox from scoring after the fly. It meant Willie would have to throw away from his body, away from the direction in which he was moving. But after his running, glove-hand catch Mays pivoted on his left foot, swung around so that for a split-second he was looking into the center-field bleachers. Spinning full-circle to the left like this consumed slightly more time than if he had been able to throw facing the diamond, but it left him in a stronger throwing position, and this is where his baseball intuition showed most clearly. Willie fired the ball. Whitey Lockman, standing in the cut-off spot, saw that it was on target and stepped aside to let the ball go through. Wes Westrum, waiting at home, caught the throw and nailed Cox sliding in.

Time magazine named this "The Throw." Chuck Dressen, the Brooklyn manager, could only shake his head and murmur, "He'll have to do it again before I'll believe it." And that other indomitable Dodger, Jackie Robinson, declared that it was the greatest throw he had ever seen. Willie was selected as Rookie of the Year for 1951.

He was off to a good start, and his baseball prospects for 1951 seemed bright indeed until something in his mail reminded him of his age and his obligation to his country. After thirty-four games in the new season Mays was called by the draft and began a twenty-one-month tour of duty in the United States Army. Most of this time he was assigned to the physical training department at Fort Eustis in Virginia, where he played with an Army baseball team. While this was not the big leagues, it was baseball, and Willie Mays was born to play ball. He played Army ball as he had played sandlot and bush league, minor league and major, fading back in the outfield or coming up fast, streaking around the bases with cap in the air or bouncing out of the dug-out with a *say hey* on his lips.

It was while playing in the Army that Willie worked out the idea behind his famous breadbasket catch, which later became a familiar Willie Mays trademark, along with his flying cap. Getting the ball back to the infield as quick as possible, he had noted, was of great importance in playing center field in the big leagues. He had observed that most outfielders hold the ball back of their ears as a starting position. He, however, was inclined to be sidearmed, to start his throws lower down and farther out from the body. This being the case, he figured that if he could make his catches at waist level with thumbs out, rather than chest high with thumbs in as the others did, he could save a fraction of time. It seemed to work, so he kept it, and when he came out of the Army, twenty months and 180 baseball games later, fans saw it for the first time in the major leagues.

Meanwhile the Giants, who had come from behind, caught the Dodgers and won the championship after Willie Mays joined them in 1951, slipped to second place after he left them in 1952 and fell to fifth place while he was away in 1953. Under the circumstances it is not surprising that the team as well as the fans awaited his return with more than ordinary anticipation. Discharge papers in hand, Willie showed up at the Giants' spring training camp in Phoenix, Arizona, on the fifth of April, 1954. On opening day of that season at the Polo Grounds he celebrated his return and delighted his fans by hitting a tie-breaking home run in the sixth inning, giving the Giants a one-run victory over their old rivals the Brooklyn Dodgers.

This opening-day homer by Willie proved to be a happy omen. The Giants, as expected and predicted, perked up after his return, won their league's pennant by a comfortable margin and followed this with a triumph in the World Series; and through the whole campaign the amazing Willie Mays simply glittered. He batted in 110 runs. Though he did not break Babe Ruth's home run record, as some overeager fans began to hope, his 41 homers that season was a proud accomplishment, especially when considered along with his total record. His 81 extra base hits set a record. And he posted the highest batting average in either league.

At the end of the season Willie was named Most Valuable Player in the National League, and the Major League Player of the Year. Topping even these recognitions in a year filled with outstanding athletic achievements, including the first four-minute mile by man in a track event, the Associated Press poll voted him Male Athlete of the Year. A New York advertising agency, measuring Mays's value by the number of demands for his name and services, reported that Willie had "become the hottest thing for us since Babe Ruth." And *The New York Times Magazine* called him, quite seriously, "Nature Boy," adding that "in a dour age, Willie Mays fulfills the specifications of Jean Jacques Rousseau (the French philosopher) in temperament and Leo Durocher in talent."

Even so, the tendency of some fans to say "as Willie goes so go the Giants" was not quite accurate. He had become and he remained important to the team, but he was not the whole team, and in the decade that followed that glorious 1954 season the Giants were sometimes on top and sometimes not, but Willie continued to give the game he loved his brilliant best. By 1963, still with the Giants, though the team had moved from New York to San Francisco and their old rivals the Brooklyn Dodgers had moved to Los Angeles, he was more than a great star. He was a personality and a legend. His

$105,000 per season also made him the best-paid baseball player in the game.

Branch Rickey, a grand old man of baseball, once called Willie the "greatest fielder that ever lived." Leo Durocher, pointing out the things in which a ballplayer may excel—hitting, fielding, running, throwing, reactions—concluded that Willie was great in all and accordingly rated him the "best player of our time." The magazine *Sport* put it about the same in 1963 in naming Mays the greatest player of the decade. Meanwhile, a rival team in the major leagues was said to have offered a million dollars for the Willie Mays contract in 1957.

Touching was an expression that came from schoolchildren in a small Pennsylvania town. Asked who in the world they would rather see, they voted overwhelmingly, Willie Mays. They were all blind.

But it has been left to Alvin Dark, Willie's old teammate and later manager with the Giants, to point out that you do not rate Willie Mays as a ballplayer. You rate players like Mickey Mantle, Stan Musial and Roger Maris, but not Willie. Willie is in a class by himself.

Casey Stengel, managing the mighty Yankees to pennant after pennant and leading the American League All-Stars against the Nationals, noticed that in a game in Candlestick Park in San Francisco all the other All-Stars on both teams were bothered by the wind and the tricks it did with fly balls. But not Willie. Willie Mays seemed to know by instinct even the velocity of the wind.

A poetic sportswriter coined a definition: "Happiness," he wrote, "is Willie Mays bringing home a run."

JESSE OWENS

[1913–   ]

Just two months after Max Schmeling knocked out young Joe Louis before an amazed crowd in Yankee Stadium, 110,000 spectators stood in the rain in Berlin, Germany, during the fading hours of the 1936 Olympics, and gave a thunderous ovation to another brown American. His name was Jesse Owens, and Arthur Daley, commenting on the event in *The New York Times*, said, "Owens was so matchless in his sheer grace and speed that his like may never be seen again." LeRoy Atkinson, another sportswriter, said, "Owen's feat in the 200-meter final in that August twilight in Germany was one of the most amazing achievements in the art of foot racing." But Chancellor Adolf Hitler, sitting with other Nazi officials in the section reserved for them, twitched uncomfortably and made a point of not congratulating or shaking the hand of the thrilling runner, as he had done with earlier winners in the games. Neither the gesture nor the explanations of his spokesmen appeared to have the effect he intended, however.

Part of the wonder of this race in the rain lay in the fact

that Owen's time for the 200-meter distance around one curve was 20.7 seconds, a world record. Never before in sports history had a runner done it in less than 21 seconds. Even more astounding, however, was the fact that this performance represented the Buckeye Bullet's eleventh world record in fourteen appearances. Remembering this, the statements by Daley and Atkinson begin to sound more like calm fact than emotional outburst.

Interestingly enough, the road to world fame and sports glory began for Jesse Owens near the place where it began for Joe Louis. He too was born on a tenant farm in Alabama and was one of seven children. His given name was James Cleveland Owens, and as a child he worked in the cotton fields near Decatur. He was small for his age in those days and so shy he did not always make himself understood when he spoke. When he entered grade school and the teacher asked his name, he answered, "J. C. Owens." Up to that time everybody, including his parents Henry and Emma Owens, had called him simply "J.C." But the teacher misunderstood and put it down as "Jesse," and since he was too bashful to correct the teacher on his first day in school, Jesse became his name from then on. Perhaps it was just as well.

About the time that the family of Joe Louis Barrow was moving to Detroit, the parents of Jesse Owens decided to pack up and head for Cleveland. That was in 1924, and Jesse, who had been born September 12, 1913, was just going on eleven. He was still small for his age, however, and his mother was almost afraid to let him go to Fairmount Junior High. He was also far behind the other children of his age in his books. In the community his family had just left, school terms were short for country folk, and the teaching was below standard. Neither of these disadvantages discouraged the youngster, however.

By the time he was fourteen, he had caught up with the kids of his own age in his studies and was more worried about an afternoon job that would help him earn money for shows and other small expenses than about his books. His family had not found it easy to make ends meet in Cleveland especially after the depression started and the father lost his foundry job. There was nothing at all for extras. The few movies Jesse managed to see had to be paid for by money he earned scrubbing kitchen floors. He had three kitchens that he mopped occasionally, but his first steady job was at a shoeshine stand.

Jesse had been hanging around the stand hoping for an opportunity when finally the proprietor decided to give him a chance. First, however, the owner insisted on talking to the youngster's mother and getting her permission. Despite Jesse's urging, this was not given without hesitation, and when his mother finally agreed to talk to the proprietor at the stand, she made a few things plain.

"I'm going to let you have my Jesse," she is reported as saying. "But I don't want him punched around. If he gets ornery just let me know and I'll paddle him."

She was a positive woman, and neither Jesse nor the owner of the shoeshine stand took her words lightly. But her fears were unnecessary, as things worked out. Jesse was a first-rate shoeshine boy, and the boss was happy with his service. In between times Jesse watched the cobbler work and taught himself to mend shoes. He even began dreaming of a time when he would own a shoeshine and repair shop of his own.

At Fairmount Junior High, however, other things were going on. Charles Riley, a gaunt, middle-aged math teacher, who organized playground activities on the side, put a notice on the bulletin board in the gym. He also posted it in the lunchroom and had it read in the classes. It invited all boys to come out that afternoon for track tryouts. And since it was spring, and since going to the tryouts meant being excused half an hour earlier from math or English, most of the boys at Fairmount went. Even those who did not expect to win were glad for the opportunity to get out and watch the others.

Tryouts were held on the sidewalk in front of the school. While they continued, one could occasionally see teachers and girls finding convenient excuses to come to the front windows and watch. Even the people in the offices showed interest, coming to the front door and standing on the steps. The janitor and his helpers and all the lunchroom helpers found out what was going on and came out.

The sidewalk had been swept clean, with chalk markings to measure the distances. Boys who had been designated as officials stood around checking their stop watches. The weather was fine, but the coach did not come out right away. First one of his assistants appeared, called off the names of contestants and started the preliminary races. One by one, the short races were ticked off and the eliminations made. When Coach Riley finally appeared to read the names of the finalists, an unknown, inconspicuous and undersized newcomer was among them. He was an underclassman named Jesse Owens. To members of his class and some of the other spectators it was exciting to see one of their number staying in there with the upperclassmen and running against the biggest and best runners at Fairmount, but they did not expect anything more. His competitors in the last race were both veterans and former winners of these events. They were the reigning champions of the school.

By the time the three runners got down on the mark, school had been dismissed, and pupils and teachers lined the front of the building. Not many expected the slender Jesse to win, but many shouted encouragement. Then when one of the older boys jumped the gun, Jesse's freshman classmates became noisy, claiming that he should be penalized and set back a yard or two.

Coach Charley Riley did not go along with that. He calmly pardoned the overanxious runner and set the three on the mark again. Then the gun fired, and the three, Fairmount's fastest, bolted forward. Unfortunately for Jesse, or so it seemed for an instant, he got a bad start. In so short a race one step lost at the beginning could make a lot of difference. On this bright afternoon, however, on the clean sidewalk in front of Fairmount High, it was not decisive. Young Jesse promptly caught his proper stride and was soon running abreast of his rivals. Nearing the finish, he pulled away, and daylight showed between him and them as he broke the tape.

Coach Riley squinted as he looked his stop watch. He could scarcely believe his eyes. The time was ten seconds flat, a junior high school record.

The excitement this caused at Fairmount was tremendous. Nobody who was there at the time every forgot it. In fact, Jesse did not let them forget it. Nor did Coach Charley Riley. He took the exciting young runner in hand that very afternoon. The two became lasting friends as well as pupil and teacher, and this friendship deepened as Riley discovered the athlete's other qualities. He admired Jesse's sense of fair play. He was impressed by the spirit he saw as the boy won nine out of ten sidewalk dashes with apparent ease but did not fret about the one he lost. He began to work seriously with Jesse, and Jesse responded by training hard. Indeed, he attained such excellent condition and form that people who saw him run sometimes complained that he did not seem to be trying hard. When his time was clocked and the records posted, they got their answer.

Interestingly, as Jesse Owens went from Fairmount Junior High to East Technical High School in Cleveland, Charles Riley went to East Tech as coach, and the personal concern of the teacher for his promising protégé continued. Under Riley's coaching Jesse went to the starting mark seventy-nine times in high school competition. He won seventy-five of these races. Neither coach nor the young sprinter offered an excuse for the four times he failed to break the tape first. None was needed. Two of the losses came while he was a sophomore competing against juniors and seniors. The other two were lost in Ohio State Interscholastic finals in competition against the best high school sprinters in the state.

Jesse also lost three other races while still a high school student. These came in the tryouts for the 1932 Olympic Games scheduled to be held in Los Angeles. He was a junior at East Tech at the time, and two of these three losses were to the great Ralph Metcalfe of Marquette University. Not only did Metcalfe take the measure of the high school flash from Cleveland that year; he went on to win gold medals in the Olympics that followed and to compile a record

as a sprinter second only to that of Jesse himself in
the overall. He was still running well, still offering a formidable challenge in the dashes four years later when the
Olympics were held in Berlin. Indeed, it was none other than
this same Ralph Metcalfe who pushed Jesse to his record-
equaling time and finished second to him in the 100-meter
dash, one of the memorable races witnessed by Hitler, his
uncomfortable cohorts and some 100,000 cheering spectators.

At the time of the 1932 tryouts, however, being on the
same starting line with Ralph Metcalfe was almost too wonderful to be true. Jesse still had another year of high school
ahead, a year that included one afternoon of undreamed
glory. It occurred in Soldiers Field, Chicago, on June 17,
1933. The occasion was the National Interscholastic championship meet. Jesse Owens and Coach Riley were there from
East Tech, and Jesse was entered in three events. The fact
that he won all three against the best high school competition
in the nation was perhaps remarkable enough, but the real
wonder was disclosed when the official results were posted.
Jesse had run the 100-year dash in 9.4 seconds, equaling the
best time ever recorded for this distance by anyone. In the
broad jump his giant leap was measured at 24 feet 9⅝ inches.
No high school boy had ever jumped that far before,
few college men. Finally he ran the 220-yard dash in 20.7
seconds, close to a world record.

One writer summed this achievement up as "the greatest
one-man track-team record in the history of schoolboy
games." It made headlines and filled columns in sports pages
across the nation. In Cleveland a neighborhood celebration
was planned to welcome Jesse on his return. Strangely, how-

ever, the adulation brought no smiles to the boy's face. When somebody wondered why, Jesse did not bite his tongue.

He wished they would "stop all this soft-soaping and give my dad a job," he said bitterly.

Investigators found that Jesse had good reason to feel as he did. The Owens family was in real need, the father having lost his job as a pourer in a mould factory as a result of depression layoffs. The picture did not remain that dark for long, however, and with twenty-eight colleges trying to recruit him, he did not have much time to feel downcast that summer.

Owens had studied automotive engineering in high school, and his marks were excellent. He chose Ohio State as his university. There Riley continued to work with him during his freshman year and developed, among other things, a new starting position for him which increased the length of his first step on take-off. But meanwhile he paid his expenses at the university by working the gasoline pumps at a filling station in Columbus. Later a member of the Ohio Legislature got him a job in the state House of Representatives.

Reporting to Larry Snyder, coach of track at Ohio State, Owens promptly began a skein of record-breaking performances that sometimes bordered on the miraculous and led eventually to the Associate Press's designation of him in 1950 as the top track performer of the first half of the twentieth century. Every season was a banner year for Jesse Owens while he was at Ohio State, but two stand out as high points.

In 1935 the National Collegiate track and field championships were held at the University of Michigan at Ann Arbor. It was there that Owens made May 25 "the greatest day in track history," according to some reporters. To this strong language Arthur Daley, columnist for *The New York Times*, replied, "It's difficult to argue with them. . . . Jesse equalled the 100-yard record of 9.4 seconds. He smashed the 220-yard record with 20.3 seconds. He shattered the 220-yard low hurdles with 22.6 seconds. And he blasted the broad jump standard out of sight with a leap of 26 feet, 84 inches," the latter a record that was still standing a quarter of a century later. No other track or field record had stood so long.

The year prior to the Olympics of 1936 was marked by certain ups and downs for the Buckeye Bullet, however. In addition to the great day at Ann Arbor the ups included his marriage to Minnie Ruth Solomon in Cleveland. The downs were represented by a meet in Lincoln, Nebraska, where Jesse was beaten by Eulace Peacock of Temple University in the broad jump and finished third behind Peacock and Metcalfe in the 100-yard dash. Indeed this poor showing against his two most formidable rivals, following so closely behind his great performance at the University of Michigan, stimulated competition and made Jesse's prospects for the Olympics anything but certain.

One week before the tryout meet at Randall's Island, however, the peerless Owens served notice. The occasion was the championship meet of the National Amateur Athletic Union at Princeton, New Jersey, and he outran the powerful Metcalfe by a full yard in winning the 100-meter dash. His broad jump of 26 feet 3 inches was good enough to win easily. Indeed it bettered the listed world mark of 26 feet 2⅛ inches, held by Japan's Ghuhei Nambu.

The event at Randall's Island a week later featured some of

the same tremendous competition together with still other stars, and Jesse Owens took the measure of all in his events. The thrill of the day, perhaps, came in the 200-meter run around a turn. Coming off the bend, Jesse was fourth in the field, but he opened up with such a burst on the stretch he not only ran the competition into the ground but zoomed to a world mark for this race.

Then came Berlin and the Olympics of 1936. On August 3 Jesse Owens won the 100-meter championship in 10.3 seconds, equaling the world and Olympic record for the distance and leading Metcalfe to the tape by a yard. The following day he established a new Olympic record in winning the broad jump with a leap of 8.6 meters or 26 feet 5+ inches. In the drizzly late afternoon of the next day, August 5, Owens led Mack Robinson (brother of Jackie Robinson the baseball player) to the finish line in the Olympic and world record time for the 200-meter race around one turn. It was this victory, following his other shining performances, that brought from the spectators in the stadium the spontaneous ovation in which Adolf Hitler and his minions declined to participate.

Four days later Owens and Metcalfe, joined by Foy Draper and Frank Wykoff won the 400-meter relay in 40 seconds, equaling the world record. In all, Jesse Owens collected four gold medals at Berlin that year, and that in itself was uncommon.

A few years later, when Hitler flung down his grim challenge, Jesse Owens was still on the American team. This time his role was to help make the American soldier physically fit. Among his subsequent activities none has pleased him more than the trips he has made on behalf of his government and its image in the eyes of the world. It was after one of these, under the auspices of the United States State Department, that he was described as "one of the best goodwill ambassadors" his country had ever sent abroad.

WILTON NORMAN CHAMBERLAIN

[1936–   ]

Neither of his parents and none of his two brothers and six sisters noticed anything unusual about young Wilt till after his fourteenth birthday. Then it was that a strange thing happened. It was almost like a fairy tale. The boy who had been growing steadily but not much faster than any other boy of his age suddenly started to grow much faster. All at once, it seemed, his clothes began to be too small for him. He went down to Laneview, Virginia, to spend the summer vacation with his father's relatives, and shot up four inches between school closing in June and school opening in September. When he came home, his mother could not believe her eyes. She had to look twice to recognize him.

Wilt's parents were people of average size. His father worked as a porter for the Curtis Publishing Company, in Philadelphia, and his mother went out several times a week to do daywork as a domestic in order to help support the large family and keep up the eight-room house in which they lived. This had been the pattern of their lives in West Philadelphia as far back as Wilt could remember.

Before he began growing extra fast, Wilt had not cared much for basketball. At Brooks Elementary School he preferred rougher sports. Basketball seemed like a "sissy" game to him in those days. Football, boxing, the contact sports, appealed more. Wilt learned to play basketball, however, and when he got to Shoemaker Junior High, he found so much basketball fever in the air he soon found that he could not avoid it. Even if he had tried to resist, his size would have practically forced him into the game eventually.

Once he got started, he also played at Haddington Recreation Center after school, and there he found himself playing with kids his own size—but often much older and more experienced. It was here among players picked up from the street corners of Philadelphia that Wilt first began to find himself in basketball. These boys played the game with a ruggedness and skill that almost swept Wilt off his feet, but he learned fast, and he gained a lasting respect for their talents.

Still shooting upward, Wilt's height reached six feet eleven inches by 1952, the year he finished Shoemaker and moved up to Overbrook High School in Philadelphia. By then, one might say, Wilt knew he belonged to basketball. He was playing for Overbrook when Jack Ryan of the Philadelphia *Bulletin* gave him the now famous and perhaps never-to-be-forgotten name "Wilt the Stilt." Wilt did not like it much, but what could he do when everybody else did?

Meanwhile, he had to do more than just play basketball at Overbrook High. Wilt's favorite subject was math. He took algebra, both the courses in geometry, trig and statistics and made B's in all of them. His memory was good, and this showed in his other subjects as well, but the record he made in basketball was better than good. In his three seasons at Over-brook Wilt scored 2,252 points. While this represented a lot of basketball for a high school student who was not neglecting his studies, it was not enough to satisfy the love Wilt had for the game. Playing with independent leagues and teams at the same time, he found opportunities to meet and play with and against talented future stars such as La Salle's Tom Gola, Pennsylvania's Ernie Beck and Temple's Guy Rodgers. Sports fans over the whole country began to hear about Wilt, the high school star at Overbrook.

He had not been at Overbrook long when he heard about a summer league in the Catskills, where basketball players could get jobs, working in the resort hotels and playing basketball on the side. This sounded good to a boy in a family the size of Wilt's, whose father's earnings were just sixty dollars a week. After his first year at Overbrook Wilt was given a job at Kutsher's Country Club. He saved his money, and in his junior year he bought a secondhand Oldsmobile for seven hundred dollars.

That secondhand Olds was important to Wilt. It marked the beginning of a hobby that has continued to interest and sometimes excite him: cars. Two years later he used his summer savings to buy a '51 Buick. This cost him six hundred dollars plus his Olds turn-in, and by this time cars were playing a definite part in the life of the tall athlete.

Running the cross-country race with the track team also interested Wilt as a high school student, but he soon decided to save his best efforts for basketball. It was not that he enjoyed one of the sports more than the other, nor that he was actually any better at one. Wilt sometimes thought, in fact, that he might have done even better at track had he chosen to concentrate on it. With his mathematical mind, however, and from bits of information he was able to pick up, it was not hard to calculate that there was little money that a track star could make from that sport in later years compared to the income from professional team sports such as basketball.

Wilt was not the only person looking ahead to his professional career while he was still at Overbrook High. Eddie Gottlieb, owner of the Philadelphia Warriors of the National Basketball Association, persuaded the professionals to pass a special rule making high school players subject to what is called "territorial rights." This is the regulation which allows the professional team in the region where the college athlete plays and perhaps makes his greatest reputation to have first chance when the time comes to sign him up as a professional. Gottleib, it seems, had spotted Wilt's pro possibilities and found out that Wilt did not expect to attend a Pennsylvania college. He was pushing the high school rule in order to keep this advantage.

Before he got action on the provision, however, he had to meet some opposition from the coach of the Boston Celtics. Red Auerbach thought Wilt might be a good enough student to make the grade at Harvard, but it was plain that Auerbach was more interested in getting Wilt for the Celtics after his college days than in getting a Harvard education for Wilt.

None of this maneuvering actually concerned big Wilt at this time, of course. In addition to the B average he was trying to maintain in his studies at Overbrook, the points he was scoring for the basketball team and the marks he was making in track, he now had the bigger job of trying to decide on a college. This was made harder rather than easier by the fact that more than two hundred colleges contacted him and expressed interest in having him as a student. According to Wilt's count, 77 major schools got in touch, about 125 minor colleges. At least two major colleges asked, through coaches or alumni representatives, if he would be interested in being the first Negro to play on one of their teams. Wilt's answer to them was, "I'd rather be the second."

These expressions of interest by the colleges began in his second year at Overbrook. The contacts were generally made by alumni or friends of the colleges. They would write or telephone or come to the Chamberlain home to talk. These continued for two years, and most of them offered the same thing: a cost-of-living scholarship. This included board, room, tuition, books and whatever incidental money the conference to which they belonged permitted. Some required that he would have to be given a job.

While the colleges were trying to appeal to him, Wilt received some very good impressions, and some not so good. The campuses, the athletic programs and the lists of their famous or wealthy alumni were always shown or described to him at their best, and some seemed almost too good to be true. Wilt enjoyed their hospitality, but he was disappointed that more of them did not say something to him about *education*, and he quickly eliminated from consideration all but a handful.

To begin with, he had made up his mind to attend a major college, his athletic interests and prospects being what they were, and this immediately scratched the 125 or more smaller colleges from his list. Next he drew a line through all the schools in the East. He had grown up in a big city, and he wanted to try life a little farther away. All of the South and the Southwest were eliminated next. These regions did not attract him for one reason or another. Likewise he crossed off the Far West, but for another reason, and in this he later confessed he had made a mistake. Somehow or other he had gotten the impression that the grade of basketball played out there was not up to the best in other sections. This, he was later to learn, was not true. Nevertheless the misapprehension helped him to further reduce his list, and he ended the first phase by settling on the Midwest as the region he would favor.

Even then, the range of possibilities remained large. Wilt's reasoning when he checked off Notre Dame and Michigan State, both of which made moves in his direction, was cool and unsentimental. You might call it hardheaded. He figured that both of these schools emphasized football more than basketball, and that this would be a slight disadvantage. This left just four colleges on the list from which he decided to make his final choice.

Dayton sounded like a good possibility, and a wealthy Ohio man who contacted Wilt made it seem very attractive. He promised to treat Wilt like his own son, should he wish to attend the University of Dayton. Wilt was interested enough to visit the campus, but he lost all interest when he ran into his first experience with racial segregation in a Dayton hotel. The Ohio man, a true Buckeye, then offered to be equally helpful if Wilt were to make either Ohio State or the University of Cincinnati his choice. So great was this individual's interest, in fact, that the NCAA became concerned and had its representatives spend four hours questioning Wilt at Overbrook about offers or inducements he may have been receiving from college recruiters or other interested parties.

The final three on Wilt's list of possibilities were Michigan, Indiana and Kansas University, and when it reached this point, he began making return visits to the prospective campuses. He liked to fly and he enjoyed the trips. Round-trip plane tickets would be left for him at the Philadelphia airport whenever a visit was scheduled, and when he arrived at the destination airport, there would be representatives from the university to meet him, transport him to the campus and give him a guided tour. Usually this turned out to be on a weekend when there was plenty of athletic activity.

All told, Wilt visited the University of Michigan twice and Indiana and Kansas three each, and for a long time he thought Indiana would be it. He noticed the way Negro athletes were received there. Two friends of his who happened to be attending at that time exerted some influence too. One was Milt Campbell, the football and decathlon star. The other was Wally Choice, a basketball ace. But somehow Wilt could not rule out K.U.

In the course of his three visits to that campus he met three Negroes whose opinions he respected and whose eagerness to have him attend Kansas made an impression on him. Dowdal Davis, the general manager of the Negro newspaper called the Kansas City *Call*, had himself been a student of the university; and the same was true of Etta Moten, a concert singer. Lloyd Kerfords, the third, had sons who had attended and become enthusiastic alumni. Mr. Kerfords owned large limestone caves which were used by the government for the storage of many kinds of surplus material. He seemed to be a man of wealth. All of them assured Wilt that he could help his race by attending K.U.

Meanwhile, Dr. Forrest C. (Phog) Allen, the famous Kansas basketball coach for whom the big new field house Wilt saw being erected on the campus was named, came to visit the Chamberlains in Philadelphia and made a lasting impression on young Wilt by his encyclopedic knowledge of the game of basketball. Nearing the retirement age of seventy, he seemed as anxious to have Wilt come to K.U. as if he were a young coach just beginning to make a reputation, but he did not limit the conversation to sports. He also talked about education, and the same was true of Professor Calvin Vanderwerf, a distinguished chemist and member of the K.U. faculty, who happened to be lecturing in Philadelphia. He used the occasion to pay a visit to the home of the Chamberlains and to say a good word in favor of Kansas as a possible college for Wilt. The fact that he was the only member of a faculty not connected with the sports program of his institution to show interest in Wilt as a prospective student may have been the deciding factor.

In May of 1955 Wilt let it be known that he had chosen K.U. The aid he had been promised was the regular Big Eight limit of board, room, tuition and fifteen dollars a month for laundry and incidentals. The fifteen dollars had to be worked out by performing some kind of work, such as selling programs at football games. Considering the spirited competition that had been worked up among college recruiters for the privilege of enrolling the tall athlete, it is not surprising that some were disappointed and perhaps let down when he made his choice. Some even wondered if anything special, over and beyond what was proper for colleges to offer a promising high school athlete, had been promised to Wilt in order to influence his decision. As a result, Wilt again was questioned at length by the NCAA in their headquarters in Kansas City. His answers must have satisfied them.

Wilt began his college work that fall with the intention of majoring in accounting, and his grades were adequate; but the attention his great height and his basketball talents had already drawn soon began to have an influence on his plans for a career. While playing out his freshman season, steadily improving his game and at the same time making K.U. students and fans impatient for the time when he would be eligible to play with the varsity, he also went out for track, as he had done at Overbrook. He qualified in the shot-put and the high jump and, in fact, did well in so many track and field events that there were those who suggested he might have been a star in the decathlon, but Wilt had already made a firm decision where track was concerned.

When the freshmen played the varsity at the end of the 1955–56 season there were 10,000 fans in the Phog Allen Field House to see Wilt in action. He did not disappoint them, and the freshmen won as expected. That fall, in his first varsity game as a sophomore, Wilt scored fifty-two points against Northwestern University, and this, as one sportswriter noted later, set the tempo for his college career. Students began calling him "The Big Dipper," a name that pleased Wilt so much more than the earlier "Wilt the Stilt" that he had it put on the bumper of his Olds. In his first season of varsity play at K.U. he led his team to the finals of the NCAA basketball tournament. In that climax game Kansas fell to North Carolina 54–53, in two overtime periods.

All told, Kansas won forty-two of fifty games the basketball team played during Wilt's two years on the varsity. His personal average was thirty points a game. He was named All-American both years. But he was not satisfied. It was not that thirty points a game did not represent a creditable showing. It was the way the opposing coaches had met his challenge. They were assigning two, three and sometimes four players to guard him. Wilt found no fault with this in itself. It was .the obligation of the opposing team to try to stop him. What troubled him was this style of play. Was it basketball? Wilt began to wonder if playing against this kind of game strategy was helping to make the all-round development as a player that would be needed later in professional basketball.

He pondered his question long and seriously before making a decision, and when he finally made up his mind to drop out of college at the end of his junior year, the news became one of the big sports stories of 1958. Wilt gave his reasons in an exclusive article in *Look*, but newspapers everywhere picked it up. Yes, it was true, he said. He was leaving college. He knew that people would speculate and wonder, but he assured readers it was not because of grades. Despite all the time and energy he was giving to basketball, track and a disc jockey show he was doing on station KLWN in Lawrence, he had still managed to maintain a grade average of C or better. There was no question but that he could have stayed on and graduated at K.U.

Nor was he unaware of the rule that prevented him from playing in the NBA until his college class graduated. That meant he would have a year to wait, but Wilt figured he could make better use of that year and improve himself more as a future professional by playing with the Harlem Globetrotters than by another season of such college competition as he had begun to face. The Globetrotters, being an independent professional team of Negro players, owned by Abe Saperstein, were not bound by the National Basketball Association's league regulation with respect to signing college players. What is more, Saperstein was prepared to pay Wilt $65,000 to play a season with the Globetrotters while waiting for him to become eligible to join the Warriors in Philadelphia.

In June of 1958 Wilt signed a six months' contract with the Trotters, to begin in October. He volunteered, however, to start playing eight weeks earlier and went to Europe to join the team for an exhibition tour against an all-star group that traveled with them. The Trotters with Wilt played thirty-five games, mostly one-night stands and mostly against their traveling companions, in Spain, Portugal, France, Germany, Switzerland, England, Belgium and Italy. London and Paris kept them for a week each, and everywhere tall Wilt, now seven feet and one-sixteenth inch, was the center of attention. In few of the smaller cities they visited had the inhabitants ever seen a seven-foot man before. In Bologna Wilt was strolling quietly when he turned around and discovered that three hundred people were following him, their mouths wide with wonder. Saperstein had several players whose height was more than six feet six, and he encouraged them all to walk about in the towns as Wilt was doing and let the people see them. In some of these places Wilt heard the Globetrotters spoken of as "the giants."

The final two weeks of the tour were spent in Russia, where the Globetrotters' exhibitions came under the heading of a cultural exchange. Here interest in the visiting Trotters reached a climax. The crowds that greeted them ran into thousands, and the seriousness of these people about athletics as well as the cordiality of the average Russians made an impression on Wilt. "A tremendous crowd of people met us with flowers at the airport," he wrote. "They were warm, personable and friendly, and we thought they'd yank our hands off with their characteristically vigorous shakes."

He was also impressed with the athletic ability they showed at the clinics conducted by the Trotters for those who had just recently learned the game of basketball.

Meanwhile, Wilt himself learned much more about basketball while playing with the Globetrotters, developed his hook shot and improved his dribbling and passing. But the financial reward was the best part of the experience. Saperstein paid Wilt a $9,000 bonus in recognition of his value to the team, and Wilt was able after taxes to buy his mother a $35,000 home on Cobber's Creek Parkway in Philadelphia, so that for the first time in his life she was able to stop going out as a cleaning woman. He was in a position to support his father too, but the father decided to keep his $60-a-week job as handyman.

Wilt was also able to do something special for himself. He bought an $8,000 white convertible. He also bought as many suits and overcoats and shoes as he needed. But the car hobby that had been with him since his junior year at Overbrook was the most exciting, and he felt that this convertible was a fair reward for 224 exhibition games with the Globetrotters in the United States and in Europe.

The following summer he made a trip back to K. U. to see if there was any way he could still finish his college work and get his degree. By then, Wilt was talking contract with Eddie Gottlieb, owner and general manager of the Philadelphia Warriors, and weighing his offer against one Saperstein had made. Saperstein was prepared to almost double the salary to get Wilt back with the Trotters again, but the offer Wilt received from Gottlieb was satisfactory and he promptly signed the contract. So when the university people at Kansas looked at the Warrior playing schedule, they advised Wilt to try to get the courses he needed at Temple or some other college nearer his home base. But that did not seem to work out either.

Wilt joined the Warriors for the start of the 1959–60 season. Not many weeks later a sportswriter for *Time* said in the February 22, 1960, issue: "Last week Chamberlain was well on his way to smashing every record on the books. Even with 14 games still to play, he had scored more points and snared more rebounds than any other player ever had in a full season. . . . To stop Chamberlain, the pros have tried every trick in the book. They may double-team him (one man in front, one behind) with the hope of blocking off passes. When Chamberlain does get the ball, the defense swirls about him like a pack of hounds circling a bear at bay. Under the hoop, they beat a tattoo on him with elbow and hip."

The next month Wilt complained in an article in *Look*, "Pro Basketball Has Ganged up on Me." Nevertheless at the end of that first season Wilt was given the basketball writers'

Hy Turkin Award for Rookie of the Year, and the Sam Davis Award as the Most Valuable Player, and it was revealed that of the eleven new marks set during the season Wilt had accounted for eight of them. They included: 37.6 point average for 75 games; 2,707 points for the season; most field goals scored (1,065); and the most rebounds (1,941). Of course, he was chosen for the Eastern All-Star team.

A year later, March 1961, Dick Schaap, writing in *Sport*, took a second-season look at the tall one and reported some comments by men who had played with and against Wilt.

Guy Rodgers: "Wilt is the greatest basketball player who ever lived."

Elgin Baylor: "He's better than any man has ever been. He can run the whole game."

Bob Cousy: "He gets the points, he gets the ball and he can go all night. What else can you say?"

"Add speed, starting speed of hand and foot, to agility, stamina and strength," said Schaap, "and you have Wilt Chamberlain, a complete athlete. . . . What Babe Ruth did to baseball—changing the whole face of the game so that the home run and all it implies grew from one small factor to a dominating force—Wilt Chamberlain, now 24, has already done to professional basketball. He has revolutionized the NBA."

In the years that have followed, Wilt has continued to justify statements as strong as these. He has also gone on to demonstrate by his success in business matters that those good grades he made at Overbrook in math were not for nothing.

JAMES NATHANIEL BROWN

[1936–   ]

In the book called the canterbury tales by Geoffrey
Chaucer there is a story about a rooster named Chanticleer.
This rooster was so proud of his wonderful voice he used to
sit on a fence for hours just crowing and feeling important.
But one day when he looked down at the ground, he saw two
cunning eyes looking up at him. They belonged to a fox.
Before Chanticleer could pull himself together and fly away,
the sly fox had begun to string him along with flattery. Never
before had he heard such marvelous crowing, the fox insisted.
Wouldn't Chanticleer please crow some more. Overcome by
the praise, the cock stretched his neck and filled the air with
one of his finest crescendos. As he did so, he closed his eyes, as
singers sometimes do, and in that instant the fox leaped upon
the fence and grabbed him.

With Chanticleer in his mouth the fox headed for the
woods. This naturally caused commotion in the barnyard,
and the cock's admirers—hens, dogs, cows and people—
screeched and screamed and ran after the abductor. They followed him to the edge of the forest. But before plunging into

the thicket the fox paused to look back at his hopelessly out-distanced pursuers. This gave the cock time to make a quick suggestion. Since the fox had so easily outrun his enemies, why not make a little fun at their expense before disappearing among the leaves and underbrush? The fox's eyes brightened. He could not resist the temptation. As he opened his mouth to taunt the barnyard folk, however, Chanticleer flew away.

Both rooster and fox had been tricked by flattery.

When Jim Brown read this story in school, he almost laughed out loud. Chaucer soon became one of his favorite authors. This may have been because the Chanticleer story sounds so much like one of the animal tales familiar to folk in his native Georgia. On the other hand, it could have been because Jim, like the author of "The Nun's Tale," in which the Chanticleer story appears, had just begun to learn something about the dangers of flattery.

The sports career of the man who has been called the king of running backs of modern times—and possibly of all time—began at Manhasset High School on Long Island. Statistics do not always tell the whole story where a great athlete is concerned, but in the case of Jim Brown they are worth mentioning. As a senior at Manhasset, Jim averaged 14.9 yards a carry on the football field. He scored 38 points per game for the basketball team. He set a school high jump record when he cleared the bar at six feet three inches. In baseball he sometimes played first base, sometimes pitched. All told, he collected thirteen athletic letters, a statistic which did not fail to catch the eye of college recruiters and coaches.

Expressions of interest and offers of scholarships began pouring in. Jim received no less than forty-five of them, but he accepted none. Instead he went to Syracuse University without an athletic scholarship but with the encouragement and financial support of a group of people in Manhasset sometimes referred to as the "committee of thirty."

Actually there is a story behind Jim Brown's choice of a college that has not been repeated often, and there are details barely hinted at in accounts of the gloom and near-discouragement that marked his freshman year on "the hill." One would never guess it, listening to the articulate and sometimes eloquent Brown lecture coaching clinics or speak at athletic banquets or school assemblies, but here is his own confession, as he looked back on his high school days:

"I never paid much attention to the books. My mother used to get after me about it, but you know how kids are; all I was interested in was playing."

As a result, Jim flunked the Syracuse entrance examination. No one who knew him well could believe he was not capable of handling college work, however, and apparently someone convinced Chancellor William P. Tolley that he should be given a chance. He was admitted "on condition."

What this did to the pride of a boy like Jim can only be imagined. For one thing, he began to reflect more seriously on the importance of a rounded education in the kind of life he wanted for himself after his playing days ended, and his very thoughtfulness may have looked to many people like despondence or moodiness. In any case, the "committee of thirty" and others interested in the prospects of Manhasset High School's most exciting athlete began to speculate. Had something gone wrong? Some professionally trained observers began to speak about the boy's "natural withdrawal," which they imagined was based in part on his coming from a broken home, but more significantly perhaps on his going to school in Manhasset with children of wealthy background while his own mother worked in their homes as a domestic servant.

The fact that the coaches of freshman teams at Syracuse were slow to recognize Jim's extraordinary talents was also noted. They were practically ignoring him. Had this upset the boy?

Jim Brown himself was unaware of such speculations and would not have been too concerned had he known. The things that were bothering him most were quite different, but they were also real. Nearly everyone who talked to him at Syracuse, for example, began by recalling the experience of another Negro athlete who had attended the university recently. In the insufferable tones in which well-meant but unnecessary advice is sometimes offered, they warned Jim against repeating the mistakes of his predecessor.

The boy they mentioned had been a triple-threat star in the Orange backfield and had become a campus hero. His fame had spread through the city as well, and he had never seemed to be short of money. In fact, he drove a flashy car, wore fine clothes and cut a fancy figure among the girls. But he had failed to finish college, and his playboy habits had done nothing to improve the image of the Negro athlete or student on the Syracuse campus.

To all of this Jim Brown listened without comment, but inwardly he did a slow burn every time the story was repeated. To him it sounded like insinuation. What right had anyone to assume he needed such advice? Nearly a decade later it was still an unpleasant memory as he recalled, "There was no record of my causing anyone any trouble, so why should they make such an assumption? That bothered me. I guess I was supposed to listen and smile, but I'm not the smiling type."

Nor did he smile on the day he was issued his ROTC uniform at Syracuse. Jim knew what it was to wear good clothes and to take care of them. His mother had taught him that. "I like my suits to fit me," he has said. "Everyone should watch their personal appearance. When you don't look good you don't feel good." But in the Army ROTC at Syracuse his freshman year Jim was given trousers that did not reach to his ankles. The sleeves to the coat he was issued were much too short, the belt several inches too high. The shoes, on the other hand, were at least two sizes too big.

Instead of protesting, Jim tried to swallow his pride as he marched on the drill field in oversized military shoes and undersized uniform. But there came a day when he could take it no longer, and he decided to end the buffoonery in his own way. He simply cut slits in his tight-fitting uniform. This brought immediate results. He was given orders to report to the office of Lieutenant Colonel Ernest L. Meggs, then head of Syracuse's ROTC.

Jim reported, expecting to hear the worst. One gathers that even dismissal at that time would not have made him feel much worse than he already felt. To Brown's surprise, however, the stern, dignified officer told him simply that he personally considered Jim good officer material, that he wanted only to see the potential developed.

"I thought it was a great thing that he believed in me," Jim said later. "Any time a strong person shows belief in you—

123

doesn't turn his back on you—it does you a world of good. I went to summer camp at Fort Bragg that year and surprised everybody—I made a nice record. I was proud, and from then on I applied myself. Colonel Meggs was the man really responsible for my buckling down."

Jim made average college grades, after deciding to stick out the first year, but he still failed to win all-out approval by most of the coaches at Syracuse. The coach of basketball, for example, a sport in which he later starred, is said to have expressed the opinion that Jim was an ordinary athlete who might possibly make it in football—as a lineman. The football staff seemed equally unimpressed. Only Ray Simmons, lacrosse coach and assistant in football, saw potential greatness in the boy from Manhasset High at this point, and it was he who recommended Jim for a scholarship as a sophomore.

Jim's failure to impress the coaches in his first year at college left no lasting bitterness, however. His best subject in the classroom was logic, and he did not fail to apply to his own situation some of the processes he studied. Perhaps there was some reason why the coaches underestimated him at first. Perhaps it was the way he walked. He gave the impression of being slow-moving, even indolent. It was not easy for them to see beyond what appeared to some people to be a sign of laziness. He had no choice but to be patient till he could convince them.

The sophomore scholarship was granted. Added to the encouragement he had received from Colonel Meggs and Coach Simmons, this was inducement enough to bring Brown back for the second year at Syracuse, but he made a spectacular fumble of a low pitchout against Villanova in the first football game of the season and was promptly benched by Coach Ben Schwartzwalder. Jim suspected that he might have sat there on the bench for the rest of the season had not a wave of influenza hit the team just prior to the game with Illinois. The coach was desperate for replacements when he called on Jim this time, and this time Jim Brown did not disappoint him.

Playing regularly thereafter, Jim began to feel like himself. for the first time in college, the real Jim Brown that so few people actually knew at that date.

Life for him had not begun at Manhasset High. His life had begun in a hospital on St. Simon's Island, Georgia. When his parents separated, the infant Jim had gone to live with his grandmother. He was seven when his mother, having found employment as a maid in the agreeable surroundings of Manhasset, Long Island, sent for him and began lavishing on him the care and attention that growing boys need. Nothing she could afford was denied to him, and she took special pride in seeing that he was well-dressed and learned how to take care of his clothes.

This was not always easy for a boy who loved to play as much as Jim did, but the lesson was learned, and Jim Brown attended elementary and high school with the children of the well-to-do without loss of pride. Sometimes his mother even sent him to school in a taxicab. When in high school his special talents for all kinds of sports began to be apparent, Jim was able to begin fitting things together.

Something similar seemed to happen to him after his difficult and disappointing first year in college and his mediocre sophomore year. Coach Ben Schwartzwalder has been quoted as saying that it was in Jim's junior year that "everything in

Brown fell into place."

What he was hinting at comes out clearly in statistics. In the twenty-four games of varsity football in which Jim Brown participated at Syracuse he advanced the ball 2,091 yards by rushing for an average of 5.7 yards per carry. He scored 25 touchdowns and 37 points-after for a total score of 187 points, and this does not include his performance in the 1957 Cotton Bowl. That postseason game alone, following his final year at Syracuse, would have lingered long in the memory of the television audience that saw it nationally had Jim not obscured it somewhat himself by repetition and the miracle of consistency which later marked his great running from fullback as a professional player with the Cleveland Browns.

Syracuse, as it happened, lost to Texas Christian in that torrid bowl game, marked by almost uncontrollable tension. The final score was 28–27, but of his team's 27 points Brown scored 21. Time and time again by explosive starts and sudden changes of pace, by battering thrusts or wriggling maneuvers, Jim Brown tore through the fired-up Texas Christian line till shadows fell on the Cotton Bowl. After the game he was named the most outstanding back on the field.

If the final score made the Cotton Bowl game on New Year's Day imperfect as a valedictory for Syracuse's own Paul Bunyan of running backs, another opportunity came on the eighteenth of the following May. With this in mind, perhaps, 7,500 fans showed up at Archbold Stadium for a track meet and a lacrosse game, with Jim Brown featured in both, his last collegiate athletic performances. A star of the first magnitude now, but with only two days' practice, Jim suited up for track against Colgate. By two o'clock he was in action.

His high jump of five feet eight inches was good enough to win first place. Half an hour later his discus throw was measured at 139 feet, also a first. Jim was taking his throws with the javelin when the Syracuse lacrosse team went to the locker rooms and began to dress for their match with Army. However, his 167-foot throw took second place and brought his individual score to thirteen points for the meet, the exact margin of the Orange victory over Colgate that afternoon.

He had to dash to the locker room in order to dress and be ready for lacrosse by game time. He made it with just minutes to spare, and he contributed one goal and three assists to the 8–6 victory scored by Syracuse. But there was even more to this contest than met the eye. It not only enabled the Orange to finish its lacrosse season with a handsome 10–0 record but brought Brown's record to within five points of the school's all-time season high for a player, despite his regular participation in basketball, track and football and the fact that in a number of lacrosse games he played less than half the time.

In the twilight of this long day on the field, after the crowd had left and Archbold Stadium was again empty, a member of the university's public relations staff, watching from an office window overlooking the stadium, saw Jim Brown cross the field alone, walking slowly, climb to the top of the stadium, turn and look down on the field. Twilight etched the silhouette.

Good at every sport he ever tried except swimming (in which he says he is just good enough not to drown), Jim Brown had a range of choice when the time came to choose a career. Boxing was perhaps the first possibility to be eliminated. Just fooling around with the gloves in gym classes, Jim had shown the kind of ability which the boxing coach thought might lead to a championship, but Brown brushed this aside. Later when promoters and managers began to coax him with offers up to $25,000, he was quoted as saying, "I don't like to hurt people." This may not have been exactly correct, but clearly in Jim's philosophic mind there was a great difference in the hurt which was incidental to advancing the football against opposition and the hurt that was an end in itself in boxing. On this basis he made his choice, but first he had another public appearance to make in Archbold Stadium. It was on occasion of his graduation. Spick and span in his perfectly fitting ROTC uniform, Jim Brown, class marshal, led the graduation procession into the stadium.

The All-Star game in Chicago followed in just a few short weeks, it seemed, but by then the big thing in Jim Brown's life was his professional career with the Cleveland Browns. Confident, but not overconfident, he joined the Browns in 1957 calmly determined to earn by performance the salary plus bonus at which he had been signed. Paul Brown and the assistant coaches gave Brown what help and encouragement they could, but they did not have to tell him that when he got to the practice field he would be on his own.

Big Ed Modzelewski was at that time the regular fullback for the Browns, and neither he nor the other proud regulars on the team had any intention of letting newcomers move them out of their positions without a struggle. Talking about it to a sportswriter several years later, after "Big Mo" had established himself in the restaurant business in Cleveland, he recalled what happened:

We were playing an exhibition against the Lions and he'd just come in from the All-Star game at Chicago. He didn't know the plays very well and wasn't very sure of himself. He didn't look too good so I figured, "Well, he's just another challenger." There's been others. One kid before Jim—an All-American from Colorado—was supposed to be the greatest thing since penicillin but they cut him and he went back to selling encyclopedias or something, and I kept playing fullback. So my first reaction to Jim was just that—probably another encyclopedia salesman.

Then there was another thing going against him . . . the law of the jungle. Let's face it, I had a lot of friends on the team. They'd try to hit Jim just a little harder than they normally would hit in practice. But he'd bust out of their arms, and gradually you could see them gaining respect. You could see them thinking, "Maybe he'll help us to a championship." The writing was on the wall for me, so I became his No. 1 rooter. You know, I doubt Jim ever knew the guys were hitting him extra hard.

When the same writer went back and told Jim what Modzelewski had said, Brown's smile broadened like a wave on the ocean. "No kidding?" he laughed. "I never knew that."

Big Ed spent the next three years watching Jim Brown with admiration—from the bench. When he had occasion, he gladly gave Jim the benefit of his own longer experience. How Jim responded can be gleaned from records of his first years as a professional football player. In the twelve games of the 1957 season Jim rushed for 942 yards, averaging 4.7 yards per carry and scoring 10 touchdowns for 60 points. He won two *Sporting News–Marlboro* trophies, one as leading rookie ground gainer and one as ground-gaining leader in the National Football League. Against the Los Angeles Rams that year he set a league record for yards gained by rushing in a single game with 237. This marked just the fourth time in more than fifty years of professional football that a running back had advanced the ball more than 200 yards in a game. When the time came for the United Press to pick up ballots for the Rookie of the Year, Jim Brown was the choice of twenty-eight of the thirty-two sportswriters who made the selection.

In his second year Jim improved his record in every respect. He increased his total yards gained by rushing from 942 to 1,527 and his average per carry from 4.7 to 5.9. His 18 touchdowns for 108 total points were in keeping, and a harvest of awards and honors followed. The Jim Thorpe Trophy was presented to him as the NFL's foremost star in 1958. Opposing players picked him overwhelmingly as the standout among the players they had faced, and the Philadelphia Writers Association and the United Press International named him American Athlete of the Year and Player of the Year respectively. In winning the ground-gaining title that year Jim Brown in the eighth game, surpassed Steve Van Buren's sturdy record of 1,146 with four weeks of play remaining.

When a Cleveland fan presented Jim with a set of golf clubs that year, Brown went out and played eighteen holes with a former Brown fullback, Marion Motley. As a beginner, Jim's score was 125. Before the summer was over, however, Jim came in with a four-under-par 77, prompting at least one admirer to insist that Brown "is the best all-round athlete to come along since Jim Thorpe."

Even so, Jim prefers the contact of football. "Every youngster likes to test himself against other youngsters," he says. "It's a thing you sorta grow up with." After four years and 48 games with the Browns, with 5,055 yards gained rushing for an average of 5.25 yards per carry, with 53 touchdowns and a total of 318 points to his credit, Brown told *Sports Illustrated* how he plays fullback.

With the authority of one who had mastered his game, he described his three-point stance, told how he took the hand-off and tucked it away leaving one arm free to fight off tacklers. "I realize this does not jibe with the classic notion of the fullback as a power man who wraps both arms around the ball, puts his head down and runs straight ahead. This is not wrong, but I like to think and run like a halfback, and I still prefer speed and shiftiness to straight-ahead power."

Jim Brown has been equally successful as a public relations man and as a radio broadcaster and platform speaker. In fact, some have estimated, and Jim has not denied, that he earns almost as much from his off-season work as from the top salary he commands as a player.

"I myself idolize the guy," Big Mo confided to a sportswriter in Ed's restaurant after his own retirement. "If I was a kid he'd be the guy I'd try to pattern myself after. I'll tell you," he added after a thoughtful pause, "I feel like the guy who played behind Babe Ruth."

ALTHEA GIBSON

[1927–   ]

THE FUTURE queen of tennis courts at Forest Hills and Wimbledon certainly did not look much like it when she was
growing up on the streets of New York's Harlem. In fact,
young Althea Gibson was something of a problem child.

Her habit of playing hooky from school was one of the
first to get her into trouble. Her teachers would spank her
occasionally right in the classroom hoping that this would
make her attend more regularly. When spanking did not help
and they reported the unexcused absences to her father, he
would give his daughter worse whippings with a belt on her
bare skin. There was no doubt that these hurt. They hurt so
bad that Althea was sometimes afraid to go home, and more
than once she went to the police station on 135th Street and
told them her father was going to beat her up and she didn't
know what to do.

The policemen telephoned her mother and asked her to
come get her daughter the first time this happened. Like many
poor people in slum neighborhoods, however, Althea's mother
was afraid of policemen and police stations. When she did not

show up, the sergeant sent the girl home accompanied by an officer. Her punishment that night was harder than usual, but it did not change her habit. Years later, recalling her rebellious childhood, Althea said, "I played hooky from school all the time. It was a habit I never lost. Later on, when I got bigger, my friends and I used to regard school as just a good place to meet and make our plans for what we would do all day."

Fighting was another bad habit she picked up on the streets. Sometimes the fights she got into were foolish, as when a bigger girl stopped her and said, "What are you supposed to be—tough or something? You're supposed to be bad?" and then punched her in the stomach. Sometimes they were fights to protect others, as when she saw her own uncle sprawling drunk on the steps of an apartment building while members of a young street gang stood around him and one of the boys went through his pockets.

"That's my uncle," Althea yelled, and ran down and helped the old fellow up the steps. The two were not quite out of range when something came flying through the air. It turned out to be a screwdriver, and it struck Althea just above her thumb. Bleeding, she got her uncle to his apartment and came storming down the stairs and took out after the boy who had robbed him and then thrown the screwdriver. When she caught up, fists began to fly.

"We had a fight," Althea says, "that they still talk about on 144th Street. We were both pretty bloody and bruised when some big people finally stopped it, and I guess you would have to say it was a draw."

Oddly enough, fighting did not get her into the same kind of trouble with her father that playing hooky did. Instead of punishing her, he praised her and took time to give her some pointers on how to look out for herself and make bullies and other rough characters leave her alone.

Aside from a mix-up about a rented bicycle that she neglected to return and a few other near misses, Althea's conduct did not actually get her into serious trouble until after she graduated from junior high school in 1941. How she managed to graduate then was a mystery to her. She did not feel that she had attended frequently enough to know honestly what went on in the school, so she assumed that perhaps the teachers had decided to pass her along to the next school and let the folks there worry with her for a while. She was transferred to the Yorkville Trade School.

That would have been all right, where Althea was concerned, because she could have as easily played hooky from Yorkville as from any other high school to which she might have been assigned at the time, but when she learned that a number of her friends were going to one of the downtown high schools, she asked to be changed so that they could continue to be together. Her request was denied, however, and this left a bitter taste.

She tried to hide her disappointment for a while, but the feeling became worse instead of better as time passed. Althea began staying out of school for weeks at a time, and because the truant officer would come looking for her and she feared her father would whip her, she began staying away from home too. This meant that more and more thereafter her father, mother and the truant officer were on the streets of Harlem looking for young Althea, while Althea was passing the time visiting with friends, riding subway trains, sitting in

135

movies and repeating this routine again and again.

There came a time eventually when she heard another girl speak of a place on Fifth Avenue at 106th Street called the Society for the Prevention of Cruelty to Children, where they would take in kids who were in trouble or had no place to go. The next time Althea had been away from home so long that she was afraid to return, she went to the Society and asked the woman in charge to take her in. "I'm scared to go home," Althea told her. "My father will whip me something awful."

They gave her a clean bed, and Althea was not anxious to leave when her parents came and got her the next day. Within a week she was back again under similar circumstances and remained longer. Before she went home this time, she was warned that if she had any more trouble with her parents, she would have to be sent to the girls' correction school at Hudson.

This was sobering, but Althea still did not want to return to the trade school, so she requested and was granted working papers not ordinarily given at her age on condition that she attend night school a certain number of hours a week. Even so, Althea confesses in her book *I Always Wanted to Be Somebody* that she did not keep her promise and attended night school for only a couple of weeks. Nobody came to pick her up for truancy, however, and she enjoyed working and being on her own.

She worked for several years at jobs that ranged from counter girl at the Chambers Street branch of the Chock Full O' Nuts restaurant chain to mail clerk at the New York School of Social Work, and she met some interesting people, like Sugar Ray Robinson and his wife Edna. She especially liked the job at the School of Social Work, but at that time she had not learned the dependability such a job requires; and when she played hooky from work to go to the Paramount Theatre in Times Square and see Sarah Vaughn in the stage show, she was fired. It broke her heart.

Indeed, this seemed to Althea the worst of all her misfortunes, and she had begun to think that it was just about the end of everything when, quite by accident, she was introduced to the game of tennis. Suddenly a strange and wonderful transformation began to come over her.

Back in her block on 143rd Street Althea had learned to play paddle tennis and had done well in games sponsored by the Police Athletic League. The courts on which the games were played were like tennis courts but only about half the size. They were marked off in the street, and the players used a wooden paddle instead of the gut racket used in tennis. The ball might be a regular tennis ball or it might be a sponge rubber ball. Althea had played this game well enough to win medals in competition with the best players from other play streets.

One of the people who saw her play paddle tennis was a musician who worked for the city as a play leader on his off days. His name was Buddy Walker, and watching Althea use the paddle, it occurred to him that she might be able to do equally well with a tennis racket. On a hunch, he bought her a cheap one and put her to hitting balls against the wall on the handball courts at Morris Park. She hit the ball so well that Buddy took her up to his apartment to meet his wife and daughter and to talk about this new game.

Had they been curious about her background, the Walkers might have learned that Althea and her parents had come to New York from a little three-store town called Silver, South Carolina. At the time of Althea's birth her mother and father were sharecropping cotton and corn on a five-acre farm. Both parents were rugged outdoor people, and to Althea her father looked a good bit like Roy Campanella, the famous Dodger catcher. But even strong hands like theirs could not do much with just five acres of farmland, and when harsh weather caught them, they were practically ruined. Indeed, it was a series of bad seasons that helped them decide to leave South Carolina and try their luck in New York City.

Daniel Gibson recalled that for three years running he had failed to make a profit on his farming. All he got out of the third year was a bale and a half of cotton. "Cotton was selling for fifty dollars a bale then," he said, "so I made seventy-five dollars for the year's work." He knew he would have to make a move of some kind, and when his wife's sister came down from New York to attend the funeral of another relative, he reached a decision.

He agreed to let the New York aunt take Althea home with her on the understanding that he would come up in a couple of months, find a job and later send for his wife. This was the standard pattern of Negro family migration from the southern states to the North in those days, and in the case of the Gibsons everything worked out according to plan. As in so many such families, this experience remained among them as a story they never got tired of telling.

Unfortunately, life in the North did not turn out to be heaven. At first the Gibsons were crowded into an apartment with the aunt who had brought Althea earlier. Eventually, however, Daniel Gibson got a job as a handyman in a garage at what seemed to him a big salary of ten dollars a week. "I sent for my wife and we were in business," he sometimes laughed afterward.

In time their situation improved further, and the Gibson family settled into an apartment of their own on West 143rd Street with Althea, her three sisters and her brother. It was at that address that Althea did most of her growing up, and it turned out to be a convenient location when Buddy Walker, the play street leader, decided to take her (the paddle tennis champ of the block) to the Harlem River Tennis Courts at 150th Street and Seventh Avenue to try a couple of sets of real tennis with one of his friends.

What happened on the courts that day was significant. The girl from 143rd Street more than justified the expectations of her play leader. She played more like an exciting stranger from another continent than a truant tomboy from a nearby neighborhood. Players on other courts stopped playing to watch her. One of those who watched was a Negro school-teacher named Juan Serrell, and it was he who suggested that Althea play a few games at a tennis club to which he belonged. The club employed a professional who gave lessons to junior members.

The idea appealed, of course, and soon Althea was learning the fine points of the game from Fred Johnson, a qualified instructor. Ability to hit the ball seemed to come natural to her, but she had to learn footwork and court strategy. Hardest of all for her to learn were the polite manners of the game of tennis. They seemed silly to Althea at that time, and the attitude she showed seemed arrogant to Mr. Johnson. Althea also found it hard to understand what her behavior off the court had to do with the game so long as she played well and won. What she did away from the court was none of his business, she reasoned.

The teacher thought otherwise, of course, and gradually, bit by bit, some of his ideas began to get across. The polite conduct of tennis players on the court began to make an impression on Althea. She began to notice and appreciate the clean white clothes the players wore, and before long she was falling into line with the new routine so well she scarcely seemed like the same youngster.

Her tennis lessons with Fred Johnson at the old Cosmopolitan Club began in 1941. Within a year she had won her first tournament, the girls' singles in the New York State Open Championship. The runner-up in this tournament, a white girl named Nina Irwin, it turned out, also took lessons from Fred Johnson, but their instructor seemed to recognize a certain spark in Althea's play that gave him special pleasure. Another result of her performance was that the club took up a collection to send her to the American Tennis Association's national girls' championship at Lincoln University in Pennsylvania later that year. This was a predominantly Negro competition, and Althea went to the finals, but she lost to a girl named Nana Davis.

Later on, after Althea had literally shaken the foundations of the tennis world, Nana Davis Vaughn recalled that 1942 match with humor:

"Althea was a very crude creature. She had the idea she was better than anybody. I can remember her saying, 'Who's this

140

Nana Davis? Let me at her.' And after I beat her, she headed straight for the grandstand without bothering to shake hands. Some kid had been laughing at her, and she was going to throw him out."

Apparently Althea had temporarily reverted to her old ways, but that was not to last. World War II canceled out the A.T.A. championship tournament the following year because of travel restrictions, but when it was resumed in 1944, Althea was there, and this time she won the girls' singles, as she did again in 1945. By then she had turned eighteen, and in 1946 she was eligible for the women's singles. These were played at Wilberforce College in Ohio that year, and as she had done at first in the girls' class, Althea went to the finals her first year —and lost. She lost to a Tuskegee Institute teacher named Roumania Peters. But it was not the loss itself that bothered her afterward. It was that Althea felt her own overconfidence had been her downfall. After winning the first set and losing the second, Roumania began to move about as if she were so tired every step was a strain. Althea relaxed, feeling sure of victory, and let down just enough to enable the older woman to call up her reserves of strength and experience and snatch the decisive set.

Althea's game had been impressive nevertheless, and among the people who noticed her were two who were to play key roles in her future career. Both were doctors, and both were bugs about tennis. One was Dr. Hubert A. Eaton, of Wilmington, North Carolina, and the other was Dr. Robert W. Johnson, of Lynchburg, Virginia. Whether or not these Negro tennis enthusiasts were looking ahead to the possibility of her someday playing at Forest Hills or Wimbledon is not too clear. If they had been, however, they could not have planned and directed her development with more keenness or devotion.

The first step, Dr. Eaton suggested, would be to get a scholarship for her at one of the Negro colleges of the South.

The only trouble with that, Althea reminded him, was, "I never even been to high school."

Certainly that made their problem harder, but it did not take the two doctors long to come up with another plan. Althea would go to Wilmington, live with Dr. Eaton's family during the school year, attend high school there and practice tennis with him on his private backyard tennis court. In the summer she would move to the home of Dr. Johnson in Lynchburg, travel with him in his car and play in the various Summer tournaments. Each doctor, it was decided, would take her into his home like one of their own children and take care of whatever expenses came up during the part of the year she spent with him.

The plan sounded so wonderful it frightened Althea. She was not sure how she would take to living in small towns after growing up in New York. Then there was that thing about the South. She had heard many stories that left her with an uneasy feeling, and she was about ready to pass up the whole wonderful opportunity for just this one reason when she chanced to mention the plan to Sugar Ray Robinson and Edna.

Sugar Ray became emphatic. "You'll never amount to anything just banging around from one job to another like you been doing," he said. "No matter what you want to do, tennis or music or what, you'll be better at it if you get some education."

Althea decided Ray was right, and in August of 1946 she wrote Dr. Eaton a letter saying she was ready to come to Wilmington. He wrote back asking her to be there by the first week in September. Enclosed with his letter was a coach ticket.

In Wilmington the Eaton family received Althea warmly. Mrs. Eaton introduced her to the Eaton children and their maid, showed her to the fresh clean room that was to be hers and immediately began to treat her like a relative. Of course, school was something of a problem, since Althea did not actually have enough solid credits to get her into the seventh grade, but the teachers decided to give her an aptitude test instead, and on the strength of the grade she made in this, they put her in the sophomore class and gave her a chance to sink or swim. She swam. More important, in Dr. Eaton's house, living as one of the family, she learned to obey rules and get along with people.

At school she joined the band, and later she played with a little jazz combo which earned money entertaining. Her instrument, which was bought for her by Sugar Ray, was the saxophone. Meanwhile, she worked hard on her studies and her tennis, and the very next summer she went to the A.T.A. national women's singles, turned the tables on Nana Davis and began a string of victories in that event which continued for ten years in succession. For whatever it was worth, this meant that for the decade beginning in 1947 Althea was the best woman player in Negro tennis.

These victories, she recalled in her life story, would get her perhaps three or four lines of type at the bottom of a page in the better newspapers. Some of the other papers would not even mention her triumphs at all. But after the A.T.A championships in the summer of 1949 Dr. Eaton sat down beside her as she dried her face with a towel and said suddenly, "Althea, how would you like to play at Forest Hills?"

She did not smile, because it was nothing to laugh about. All she said was, "You gotta be kidding."

"I'm not saying for sure," he added, "but it could happen. People are working on it."

"I'm ready any time they are," Althea assured him.

Sure enough, cracks began to appear in the wall. Opportunities to play in the Eastern Indoor Championships and the National Indoor Championships were offered, rather surprisingly, and each time Althea lasted until the quarterfinals, which was encouraging. She was not the first Negro who had played in these matches, for Dr. Reginald Weir had broken the ice a couple of years earlier, but she was the only one that year, and lasting until the round of eight against such star competititon as these tournaments brought out made these matches tremendously exciting for the girl from Williston Industrial High in Wilmington, North Carolina.

Another result of her play in these tournaments was a college scholarship at Florida A. & M. University at Tallahassee. Two days after her high school graduation Althea said good-by to the Eatons and caught a train going south. She began taking summer courses immediately, not waiting for her freshman year to start officially. Under the guidance of tennis coach Walter Austin and athletic director Jake Gaither she took some time out to play a few tournaments, and early in 1950 she was invited again to play in the National Indoors. This time she went to the finals before being eliminated by Nancy

144

Chaffee, the same player who had defeated her the year before. But again the experience was wonderful, and this time something was added. On the campus at Florida A. & M., often called FAMU, the reception that greeted her when she returned was almost as enthusiastic as if she had won the tournament. The school's marching band came out and played the alma mater when she stepped off the train, and someone put up a big sign which said, "Welcome home, Althea." Obviously they thought that what she was doing in tennis had a meaning over and beyond the winning or losing of games, and they were there to express this as best they could.

But where would it all lead? Back in 1950 the United States Lawn Tennis Association did not seem to be paying the slightest attention to Althea. Others were, of course, and in the July 1950 issue of *American Lawn Tennis* magazine Alice Marble, one of the greatest women tennis players America has produced, wrote an editorial which brought things to a head. Here are some quotes from her article:

I think it's time we faced a few facts. If tennis is a game for ladies and gentlemen, it's also time we acted a little more like gentlepeople and less like sanctimonius hypocrites. If there is anything left in the name of sportsmanship, it's more than time to display what it means to us. If Althea Gibson represents a challenge to the present crop of women players, it's only fair that they should meet the challenge on the courts, where tennis is played. I know those girls, and I can't think of one who would refuse to meet Miss Gibson in competition. She might be soundly beaten for a while—but she has a much better chance on the courts than in the inner sanctum of the committee (of the USLTA), where a different kind of game is played. . . .

We can accept the evasions, ignore the fact that no one will be honest enough to shoulder the responsibility for Althea Gibson's probable exclusion from the Nationals. We can just "not think about it." Or we can face the issue squarely and honestly. It so happens that I tan very heavily in the summer—but I doubt that anyone ever questioned my right to play in the Nationals because of it. Margaret du Pont collects a few freckles—but who ever thought to omit her name for such a reason? The committee would have felt pretty foolish saying, "Alice Marble can't play because of that tan," or "We can't accept Margaret du Pont; she gets freckles across her nose." It's just as ridiculous to reject Althea Gibson on the same basis—and that's the truth of it. She is not being judged by the yardstick of ability but by the fact that her pigmentation is somewhat different. . . .

Speaking for myself, I will be glad to help Althea Gibson in any way I can. If I can improve her game or merely give her the benefit of my own experiences, as I have many other young players, I'll do that. If I can give her an iota more of confidence by rooting my heart out from the gallery, she can take my word for it: I'll be there.

Encouraged by this tremendous boost, Althea immediately applied to enter the New Jersey State Championships at the Maplewood Country Club. She was refused, and for a few days her hopes wavered, but then the wall that had begun to show cracks suddenly broke. The Orange Lawn Tennis Club in South Orange, New Jersey, one of the outstanding clubs in the eastern group, accepted her application to play in the important Eastern Grass Court Championships, a tournament that ranked second only to the Nationals in the tennis circles of the Atlantic Seaboard.

The barrier was down. While Althea was not a world-beater in that South Orange tournament, she did defeat a high-ranked player in the first round before she was herself eliminated by Helen Pastall in the second, and she was off on wings to the National Clay Courts Championships at Chicago, where Doris Hart stopped her in the quarterfinals. Then it was that Althea received a message, passed along by word of mouth, that if she were to apply for entrance in the Nationals, she would be accepted. She did, and she was.

Casually, as if there was nothing extraordinary about it, the president of the USLTA announced in August of that summer that Althea Gibson was one of the fifty-two women whose entries for the national championship tournament had been accepted. But he did add, rather unnecessarily, it seemed, "Miss Gibson has been accepted on her ability."

Her play at Forest Hills that year was exciting. It brought one victory and seemed close to bringing another over the favored Louise Brough, Wimbledon champion, former champion of the United States and certainly one of the top women tennis players in the world. According to the *New York Journal American,* "a fabulous upset was in the making. But it never came about. Ten minutes of thunder and lightning finally delivered the deluge. It poured, and the match ended as players, officials and spectators scurried to cover under the stands."

Nevertheless, this tournament opened up still more opportunities, even though it did not bring a championship to Althea. In fact, several years of hope deferred were to intervene before that dream was to be realized. Meanwhile, she returned to FAMU and graduated, continued to play tennis and break barriers in tournaments around the country, and finally received an invitation from the State Department to make a tour of Southeast Asia with a team of American tennis players. The tour was a success, and Althea returned home with an international reputation.

The Althea Gibson year of 1957 was her greatest, for that was the year of championships at Wimbledon and Forest Hills, a year of congratulations by the Queen of England as well as President Dwight D. Eisenhower of the United States, a year of parades and fame, the year of the Wightman Cup and glorious championship blazers worn on newsreels and television. After the victory at Forest Hills Vice President Richard Nixon presented the trophy to Althea, and she made a little speech:

"Winning at Wimbledon was wonderful, and it meant a lot to me. But there is nothing quite like winning the championship of your own country. That's what counts the most with anybody."

INDEX

149

INDEX

ABOUT THE AUTHOR

Born in Louisiana, educated and brought up in California, Arna Bontemps first arrived in New York in the twenties, just in time to participate in the "upsurge of creativity" known as the Harlem Renaissance. Since then, he has written novels, poetry, essays, and more than a dozen books for children and young people.

God Sends Sunday, his first novel, reached Broadway in 1946 as *St. Louis Woman*, with music by Harold Arlen. His *Story of the Negro* received the Jane Addams Children's Book Award in 1956, and he is credited as "editor" of W. C. Handy's autobiography, *Father of the Blues*. With Langston Hughes, he compiled *The Poetry of the Negro* and *The Book of Negro Folklore*. A collaboration with Jack Conroy in Chicago produced *They Seek a City* and *The Fast Sooner Hound*.

His *100 Years of Negro Freedom*, which was begun in 1949 on a John Simon Guggenheim Fellowship, was published in 1961. His most recent publication, *Famous Negro Athletes*, grew from a lifelong interest in sports.

The working years of Mr. Bontemps, father of six, have also included a decade of teaching and somewhat more than that as Head Librarian at Fisk University, a position he still holds. Recently, he became the first Negro member of the newly-appointed metropolitan Nashville Board of Education.